Reminiscences of a Rebel

Wayland Fuller Dunaway

Contents

PREFACE 7
CHAPTER I 8
CHAPTER II 11
CHAPTER III 14
CHAPTER IV 16
CHAPTER V 20
CHAPTER VI 25
CHAPTER VII 29
CHAPTER VIII 34
CHAPTER IX 38
CHAPTER X 42
CHAPTER XI 48
CHAPTER XII 54
CHAPTER XIII 59

REMINISCENCES OF A REBEL

BY

Wayland Fuller Dunaway

PREFACE

Notwithstanding the title of this volume, I do not admit that I was ever in any true sense a rebel, neither do I intend any disrespect when I call the Northern soldiers Yankees. The use of these terms is only a concession to the appellations that were customary during the war.

It is my purpose to record some recollections of the Civil War, and incidentally to furnish some historical notices of the brigade to which I was attached. Here and there I have expressed, also, some opinions concerning the great events of that dreadful period, some criticisms of the conduct of battles and retreats, and some estimates of the abilities of prominent generals.

The incentive to write is of a complex nature. There is a pleasure, especially to the aged, in reviving the memories of the past and narrating them to attentive hearers. Moreover, I hope that this book will furnish instruction to those who have grown up since the war, and entertainment to older persons who participated in its struggles, privations, and sorrows. And besides, the future historian of that gigantic conflict may perhaps find here some original contribution to the accumulating material upon which he must draw. He will need the humble narratives of inconspicuous participants as well as the pretentious attempts of the partial historians who have preceded him. The river flows into the sea, but the river itself is supplied by creeks and rivulets and springs.

W. F. D.

CHAPTER I

"Lay down the axe; fling by the spade;
Leave in its track the toiling plow;
The rifle and the bayonet-blade
For arms like yours were fitter now;
And let the hands that ply the pen
Quit the light task, and learn to wield
The horseman's crooked brand, and rein
The charger on the battle field."
--BRYANT.

In the fall of the year 1860, when I was in my nineteenth year, I boarded the steamboat *Virginia*,--the only one then running on the Rappahannock river,--and went to Fredericksburg on my way to the University of Virginia. It was my expectation to spend two sessions in the classes of the professors of law, John B. Minor and James P. Holcombe, and then, having been graduated, to follow that profession in Lancaster, my native county.

The political sky had assumed a threatening aspect. The minds of the Southern people had been inflamed by the insurrectionary raid of John Brown upon Harper's Ferry, especially because it had been approved by some Northern officials, and because the surrender of some fugitives from justice, who had taken part in that murderous adventure, had been refused by Ohio and Iowa. The election of Abraham Lincoln added fuel to the flame. Having been nominated by the Republican party, he was constitutionally chosen President of the United States, although he had not received a majority of the popular vote. The election was ominous, because it was sectional, Mr. Lincoln having carried all the Northern states but not one of the Southern. The intensest excitement prevailed, while passion blew the gale and held the rudder too.

While I believed in the right of secession I deprecated the exercise of that right, because I loved the Union and the flag under which my ancestors had enjoyed the blessings of civil and religious liberty. I did not think that Lincoln's election was a sufficient cause for dissolving the Union, for he had announced no evil designs concerning Southern institutions; and, even if he had, he was powerless to put them into execution. He could have done nothing without the consent of Congress, and his party was in a minority both in the Senate and in the House of Representatives.

Before Christmas South Carolina, not caring for consequences and blind to the horrible future, passed an ordinance of secession; and her example was followed in quick succession by Mississippi, Florida, Alabama, Georgia, Louisiana, and Texas. These seven states organized the Southern Confederacy, of which Jefferson Davis was inaugurated President, February 18, 1861. In April Fort Sumter was captured, and on the 15th of that month President Lincoln issued a proclamation calling on the remaining states to furnish their quotas of an army of seventy-five thousand soldiers for the purpose of destroying the Confederate government. Two days later the Virginia convention passed an ordinance of secession. Being compelled to take sides, the Old Dominion naturally cast her lot with her Southern sisters. War had begun,--intestine war, of whose magnitude and duration no living man had any adequate conception.

These events conspired with other causes to infuse in me a martial spirit. The conviction was growing in me that, as my native state was about to be invaded, I must have a place in the ranks of her defenders. I was influenced by speeches delivered by Governor Floyd, Professor Holcombe, and Dr. Bledsoe, and still more by the contagious example of my roommate, William H. Chapman, who had gone with a company of students to Harper's Ferry, and had returned. What brought the conviction to a head was a flag. One morning in the latter part of April, as I was walking from my boarding-house to the University I saw a Confederate banner floating above the rotunda. Some of the students during the night, surmounting difficulty and braving danger, had clambered to the summit and erected there the symbol of a new nation. I was thrilled by the sight of it as if by an electric shock. There it was, outstretched by a bracing northwest wind, flapping defiantly, arousing patriotic emotion. Unable longer to refrain, I went as soon as the lecture was concluded to Professor Minor's residence and told him I was going to enter the military service of Virginia. He sought to dissuade me, but, perceiving that he could not alter my rash decision, he gave at my request a written permission to leave his classes.

But how to get home?--that had become a perplexing question. I could not go the way I had come, because the *Virginia* fearful of capture had ceased to make trips from Fredericksburg to Lancaster, and there was no railroad to that part of the state. Knowing that my uncle, Addison Hall, was a member of the Convention, I determined to take a train to Richmond and seek his advice. I felt relieved when he informed me that he was going the next morning, and that I could go along with him. We took an early train to West Point, and being ferried across the Mattaponi river, obtained from one of his friends a conveyance to Urbanna. We hired a sloop to take us to Carter's creek, and thence we proceeded in a farm wagon to his home in the village of Kilmarnock. The next morning he sent me to the home of the Rev. Dr. Thomas S. Dunaway, my brother, and my guardian.

In a few days I enlisted in a company that was being raised by Captain Samuel P. Gresham, who had been a student at the Virginia Military Institute. And thus the student's gown was exchanged for the soldier's uniform.

Before we were regularly mustered into service an expedition was undertaken that indicated at once the forwardness of our people to engage the enemy and their ignorance of military affairs. The report having been circulated that a Federal gunboat was lying in Mill Creek in Northumberland county, its capture, or destruction, was resolved upon by about a hundred men, who had assembled at the county seat of Lancaster. With no weapons except an old smooth-bore six-pound cannon, and that loaded with scrap iron gathered from a blacksmith's shop, we proceeded to Mill Creek and unlimbered on the bank in plain view of the boat, and distant from it some two or three hundred yards. I have always been glad that we had sense enough to refrain from shooting, for otherwise most of us would have been killed then and there. Seeing the hopelessness of an unequal combat, we retired from the scene somewhat wiser than when we went. In that instance was not "discretion the better part of valor"?

CHAPTER II

War, war is still the cry, "War to the knife."
                                              --BYRON.

There was in the central part of the county a beautiful grove in which the Methodists were accustomed to hold their annual camp-meetings. On account of its location and the shelter afforded by its tents it was in 1861 transformed into a rendezvous of a radically different nature, the military companies that had been raised in the county assembling there preparatory to going into the army. It was there that Captain Gresham's company, known as the Lacy Rifles, was formally enrolled by Col. R. A. Claybrook and Dr. James Simmonds. When they came to where I stood in the line of men they declined to enlist me because I appeared pale and weak on account of recent sickness. I said, "Do as you like, gentlemen, but I am going with the boys anyhow." "If you talk like that," they replied, "we will insert your name."

    Not many days afterward the company assembled at the court-house, and, having sworn allegiance to the Southern Confederacy, was duly mustered into its service. In vehicles of all sorts we drove to Monaskon wharf, where the schooner *Extra* was moored to receive us and to convey us up the Rappahannock river. As the vessel glided along what a jolly set we were!--gay as larks, merry as crickets, playful as kittens. There was singing, dancing, feasting on the palatable provisions supplied by the loving friends we were leaving, with no thought of captivity, wounds, nor death. Ignorant of war, we were advancing toward its devouring jaws with such conduct as became an excursion of pleasure. The only arms we then possessed were two-edged daggers made of rasps in blacksmith shops, and with these we were going to hew our way to victory through the serried ranks of the invading army! Ah, well! we knew better what war was after we had become the seasoned veterans of many campaigns.

When the vessel had proceeded up the river as far as Fort Lowry it rounded to, because a solid shot ricochetted before the bow, and we were transferred to the steamboat *Virginia*, which carried us to Fredericksburg. Passing along the streets, attracting attention by our neat gray uniforms, we marched out to the fair-grounds, and rejoiced to obtain the friendly shelter of the cattle stalls. They were not as comfortable as the chambers of our homes--but what of it? Were we not soldiers now? It is wonderful and blessed how human nature can accommodate itself to altered environments.

We were supplied with smoothbore, muzzle-loading, Springfield muskets, small leather boxes for percussion caps, and larger ones for cartridges. For the information of the present generation let it be explained that the cartridge was made of tough paper containing powder in one end and the ounce ball of lead in the other; and the manner of loading was this: the soldier tore off with his teeth the end, poured the powder into the muzzle, and then rammed down the ball; this being done, a cap was placed on the nipple of the breech, and the gun was ready to be fired. That musket is antiquated now, but it did much execution in former days.

Maj. J. H. Lacy, for whom the company was named, presented an elegant silk banner, which at Captain Gresham's request I received in the best language at my command. It was never borne in battle, for it was not companies but regiments that carried banners. There was but one flag to a regiment, and that was always carried in the center. Twice a day there was a course of drilling in tactical evolutions and in the handling of the muskets. At first I was hardly strong enough to sustain the fatigue, but I rapidly grew stronger under the combined influence of exercise, sleeping in the open air, and the excitement of a military life. The war did me harm in many ways, but it was the means of increasing my capacity for bodily exertion. During the encampment at Fredericksburg many of my spare moments were spent in reading the New Testament and Pollok's "Course of Time."

We did not long remain in Fredericksburg; but being transported on cars to Brooke Station we marched up to camp Chappawamsic, near a Baptist church of that name. There the Lacy Rifles became Company F in the 47th regiment of Virginia Volunteers, commanded by Col. G. W. Richardson of Henrico county, who had been a member of the Virginia Convention that passed the ordinance of secession. He was a brave and patriotic gentleman, but unskilled in military affairs; and he did not long retain the command.

From the summer of 1861 until the spring of 1862 we spent the time in company and regimental drill, and in picketing the shore of the Potomac river day and night, lest the enemy should effect a landing and take us unaware. During that time no shots were exchanged with the enemy, because no landing was attempted. The only fighting that we saw was at Dumfries where there was a Confederate fort, to which we marched to act as a support in case the Yankees came ashore. Three vessels of the Federal navy passed slowly down the river, between which and the fort there was a brief but lively cannonade; but so far as I know there was no resulting damage to either side.

On Sunday, July 21, we heard the booming of the cannon at Bull Run, lamenting that we had no part in the battle. When we afterward heard how McDowell's army skedaddled back to Washington more rapidly than they came, we thought that the war would end without our firing a gun. So little did we understand the firmness of President Lincoln's mind and the settled purpose of the North!

The winter was spent in comparative comfort, for we moved out of tents into cabins built of pine logs, each one having a wide arch and a chimney. At Christmas some good things were sent to me, among which was a dressed turkey, which I did not know how to prepare for the table, for even if I had possessed some knowledge of the culinary art there was no suitable oven. Fortunately a comrade by the name of John Cook,--an appropriate name for that occasion,--came to my relief and solved the problem in a most satisfactory manner. The bird was suspended by a string before the open fire, and being continually turned right and left, and basted with grease from a plate beneath, it was beautifully browned and cooked to a turn.

CHAPTER III

Drummer, strike up, and let us march away.
         --SHAKESPEARE'S *Henry VI*.

In the spring of 1862 Gen. George B. McClellan with an army of 120,000 men, thoroughly drilled and lavishly equipped, set out from Washington to capture Richmond from the north; but he had not proceeded far before he changed his mind about the line of advance. His forces were transported to Fortress Monroe with the design of approaching the city by the way of the peninsula that lies between the York and the James rivers. The correctness of his judgment was justified by subsequent campaigns; for the successive attempts of Pope, Burnside, Hooker, and Grant to take the Confederate capital from the north were all disastrous failures.

In order to check the upward progress of McClellan's army, Gen. Joseph E. Johnston withdrew his forces from Manassas and the shore of the Potomac and concentrated them on the Peninsula. The 47th regiment marched from its winter quarters to Richmond, and was thence transported down the James to a wharf not far from Yorktown. During our brief stay in that vicinity, the companies were authorized to elect their officers; and I, who had been acting as Orderly Sergeant, was chosen Third Lieutenant.

As the National army advanced, the Confederates fell back toward Richmond. Our regiment was not in the engagement that took place near Williamsburg on the 5th of May, but I saw then for the first time some wounded men and prisoners. The retreat was conducted somewhat rapidly, but in an orderly and skilful manner. I do not remember that we marched in darkness but once, and then we trudged all night long through shoe-deep mud. At times when the men in front encountered an unusually bad place those who were behind were compelled to come to a temporary halt. If I did not sleep while walking along I came as near to it as weary mortal ever did, and I am sure that I dozed while standing still.

General Johnston posted his army between Richmond and the Chickahominy river, the 47th regiment being on the left, not far from Meadow bridge, and in the pestilential low-grounds of that sluggish stream. Swarms of mosquitoes attacked us at night and with their hypodermic proboscides injected poisonous malaria in our veins, to avoid which the sleeping soldier covered his head with a blanket. The complexion of the men became sallow, and every day numbers of them were put on the sick-list by the surgeons.

The 47th regiment, commanded by Col. Robert M. Mayo, and having brigade connection with some regiments from North Carolina, had its first experience of real war in the battle of Seven Pines (or Fair Oaks), which was fought on the 31st of May. On that day General Johnston attacked the left wing of the Federal army, which had been thrown across to the southern side of the Chickahominy. To some persons the declaration may seem surprising, but it was with real pleasure that I went into the battle. It was the novelty of it, I suppose, that prevented me from being frightened by exploding shells and rattling musketry. The dread of these things came afterward when I saw fields scattered over with the wounded, the dying, and the dead, and among them some of my dearest friends. In that affair our Lieutenant-Colonel, John M. Lyell, was seriously wounded, and the regiment sustained a loss of about fifty men. Our chaplain, Mr. Meredith, of Stafford county, went into action with us, but while he did not do the like again, it is no impeachment of his courage. His duty lay in other directions; and it ought to be recorded in his praise that after every battle he might be found doing all he could to relieve and comfort the wounded.

CHAPTER IV

In peace there's nothing so becomes a man
As modest stillness, and humility;
But when the blast of war blows in our ears,
Then imitate the action of the tiger;
Stiffen the sinews, summon up the blood.
                    --SHAKESPEARE'S *Henry V.*

After the undecisive battle of Seven Pines the 47th regiment together with the 40th and the 55th Virginia regiments and the 22nd Virginia battalion was formed into a brigade, and this combination continued until the close of the war. It was known as the First Brigade of the Light Division, which was composed of six brigades, and commanded by Maj.-Gen. A. P. Hill. Why it was called the Light division I did not learn; but I know that the name was applicable, for we often marched without coats, blankets, knapsacks, or any other burdens except our arms and haversacks, which were never heavy and sometimes empty.

On Thursday, June 26, the memorable but miss-called "battles around Richmond" began. Being on the left of the army, the First Brigade had the honor and the danger of being the first to cross the Chickahominy. Passing over Meadow bridge, we dispersed the enemy's outpost, only one man being wounded in the passage, and hurried on towards Mechanicsville and Beaver Dam, where was posted the extreme right of the Federal army. The contest raged for six hours. We failed to dislodge the enemy from its naturally strong and well-fortified position across Beaver Dam creek, and our loss was heavy,--heavier in some other brigades than in ours. The following morning, discovering that our antagonists had withdrawn, we crossed over Beaver Dam in pursuit.

McClellan had decided to retreat! He called it a change of base; but if a change of base from the York to the James river was good strategy, why did he not do it before he was attacked? It looks very much as if he gave "a reason upon compulsion." It must be conceded that he managed the retreat with admirable ability, although, while inflicting severe punishment upon Lee's army, it involved the loss of 10,000 prisoners, 52 pieces of artillery and 35,000 stand of small arms, besides immense stores of ammunition and provisions. But why retreat? Was it for this that he had led to the gates of Richmond a grand army of brave and disciplined men, at an enormous cost to his government? Having many qualities of a great commander, he lacked the ***gaudium certaminis*** and the daring that assumes the hazard of defeat. In war the adage holds good with emphasis: "Nothing venture, nothing gain." The celebrated generals of all times, confiding in their own skill and the bravery of their soldiers, have been bold even to the degree of seeming rashness. Such was the spirit and conduct of Lee when with half the numbers he assaulted Hooker, and afterward Grant, in the Wilderness.

McClellan's army being astraddle the Chickahominy, two courses of action were open to him when he was attacked.

He might have concentrated on the north side of the river, leaving a sufficient force to guard the bridges in his rear, and then assumed a strong defensive position. Having abandoned Beaver Dam he withdrew to Gaines' Mill,--a place most favorable for defense,--still having 60,000 men in striking distance across the river. If instead of vacating that position, or suffering a portion of his army to be driven from it, he had reenforced it by a half of those unoccupied 60,000 men, I do not believe he could have been dislodged by all the valor and dash of the Confederate army.

The other line of action that he might have chosen was to concentrate on the southern side of the river, destroy the bridges, and then crushing the small army of Magruder, make a quick attack upon Richmond, while the forces of Lee and Jackson were on the other side. It seems to me that either course would have been better and nobler than the inglorious retreat to Harrison's Landing. It appeared that Lee was gaining victory after victory; but until the battle of Malvern Hill he was fighting only portions of McClellan's forces. In that engagement alone did the Union army contend with its undivided strength, and there it gained a victory. If it could hold its ground there after having suffered many losses, could it not much better have repulsed the Confederates at Gaines' Mill?

When the First Brigade advanced to the charge at Gaines' Mill, on the 27th of June, it emerged out of a wood into a large field, which declined toward a ravine through which a stream of water ran, and on the other side of which the ground rose somewhat precipitously to a considerable altitude. It had been wisely chosen for defense, and the opposite high ground was lined with infantry and crowned with batteries. As it was impossible to dislodge the enemy until some diversion should be created on one of his flanks, our men lay prone upon the ground, while bullets and shells hurtled among us and above us. At length seeing a brigade on our left rapidly advancing where the enemy's position was less formidable, we rose up and, with the inspiring "rebel yell," ran down the slope, crossed the little creek, clambered up the hill, and poured a volley into the retiring Yankees, some of whom were Duryea's Zouaves with their flaming uniforms. It was then that we more than repaid them for the loss they had inflicted upon us. On that day there fell some of my dearest friends, among whom was St. John F. Moody, who for three years had been my teacher, and afterward became my beloved companion. So patriotic and brave was he that if "Dulce et decorum est pro patria mori" ever was true of any hero it was of him.

The next battle in which the brigade took part was that of Frazier's Farm, three days later. As we entered a field we saw before us a battery (which I believe was Randell's) supported by a firm line of infantry. In Wilson's history of the war he says: "One of the most brilliant charges of the day was made by the 55th and the 60th Virginia." The correct statement is that it was made by our brigade composed, as has been said, of the 40th, the 47th, the 55th, and the 22d Virginia. We rushed across the field, drove away the opposing infantry, and captured the battery. One of the gunners lying on the ground badly wounded jerked the lanyard of a loaded cannon just as we had almost reached the battery. Happily for us the discharge flew over our heads. He knew that he was in our power, for all his comrades were fleeing away, and he had no right to fire upon us. The deed was more like vengeful murder than honorable war; however, we did him no harm, for though his spirit was spiteful his pluck was commendable.

It was late in the afternoon; and as we stood in line by the captured guns, ready to receive an expected countercharge, a lone horseman approached who proved to be Major-General McCall, who in the fading twilight had mistaken us for his own men. Hearing numerous cries to halt and seeing many muskets leveled at him, he dismounted and led his horse to where we stood. Being conducted before Colonel Mayo, he said, "For God's sake, Colonel, don't let your men do me any harm." Colonel Mayo was so indignant at the implied accusation that he used some cuss words, and asked him whether he thought we were a set of barbarians. If he had been captured in battle, I should have been glad; but, as it was, I felt sorry for him, and if I could have had the disposal of him I would have paroled him and turned him loose.

The First Brigade did not again come under fire until we reached Malvern Hill, the 1st of July. There McClellan had skilfully stationed his entire army, and all the valorous efforts of Lee's army to storm the position were unavailing. One of our men addressed a North Carolina regiment as "Tarheels" and received for answer, "If you had had some tar on your heels, you would have stuck to that battery better than you did."

McClellan, having for six days acted on the defensive, and in the last engagement having been virtually victorious, had an opportunity to assume the offensive; for in war as in the game of chess an unsuccessful attack invites defeat. On the 2d of July, if he had inspired his regiments with the cry of "On to Richmond" and attacked the Confederates unprepared for so surprising a reversal, who can tell what might have been the result? Was it not worth the trial? And if he had failed, could he not then have fallen back to the cover of the gunboats? But he was bent on going to Harrison's Landing, and thither his army retreated all night over a muddy road. Thus ended the second attempt to capture the Confederate capital.

CHAPTER V

When Greeks joined Greeks, then was the tug of war.
                    --NATHANIEL LEE.

After the battle of Malvern Hill the First Brigade had a brief and enjoyable respite from marching and fighting, while it bivouacked in the pine forest near Savage Station.

Gen. John Pope, with his "headquarters in the saddle," set out from Washington with a numerous force to capture Richmond, and was reenforced by the remains of McClellan's army that had been transported from Harrison's Landing to Acquia creek. Jackson's corps, of which Hill's Light Division was an important part, was dispatched to watch his movements and to check his progress. From the flat lands of the James and the Chickahominy we marched to the hill country, and for a few days remained near Orange Court House. On the 9th of August we forded the Rapidan in search of the enemy. A suffocating cloud of dust enveloped our toiling host, and so intense was the heat that a few of the men fell sunstruck in the road. During this march, as also on similar occasions, I saw packs of cards scattered along the highway; for though the soldier might play them for money or amusement when there was no prospect of an engagement, he did not relish the thought of their being found upon him if he should be killed. In the afternoon we encountered a portion of the National army under the command of General Banks and fought the battle of Cedar Run, in which our people were victorious. That night the hostile lines were so close that we could hear the Yankees talking, but could not distinguish the words. When daylight came they were far away.

Toward the latter part of the month Pope's army occupied a position near Warrenton in Fauquier county, while across the North Fork of the Rappahannock river he was confronted by Lee's united army in Culpeper.

To cross the river and force the Federal position by a front attack was plainly impracticable; but in some way the Yankees must be removed and compelled to fight on something like equal terms. The plan was formed that Jackson with his corps should by a forced circuitous march obtain the enemy's rear and thus, cutting the line of his communication, compel him to retire from his advantageous location, and that Lee with Longstreet's corp should rejoin Jackson and bring on an engagement with his entire army. To some military critics this division of the army in the face of an unchastised antagonist might seem to contradict the rules of sound strategy, but in the fertile minds of Lee and Jackson it was the dictate of consummate genius. Such a division occurred in Maryland, just before the battle of Sharpsburg, and again at Chancellorsville the following year, and each time it was advantageous to the Confederate arms. These two men had the utmost confidence in each other, and either felt safe while the other was making an independent movement. In the course of the years that have elapsed since the termination of the war I have frequently been asked, "Which was the greater general, Lee or Jackson?" After pondering this question for forty-five years I am yet unable to decide; and that reminds me of Abe Lincoln and the hats. When he became President, two enterprising merchants in Washington, desiring to secure his custom, each presented him with an elegant silk hat, and it so happened that they called at the same time to learn his opinion of their gifts. "Gentlemen," said Mr. Lincoln, "these hats mutually excel each other."

On Tuesday, the 26th of August, the march of Jackson's corps began, every step of the onward way bringing us nearer to the Blue Ridge where it borders the county of Rappahannock, and causing us to guess that through some gap of the mountain we were going into the valley. We did not know what Old Jack, (as he was familiarly and affectionately called,) was up to, but it did not matter what was the objective,--so implicit was the confidence reposed in his military judgment. Passing out of Rappahannock and skirting the base of the Blue Ridge, we rested for the night at Salem, in Fauquier, a station of the Manassas Gap Railroad, the name of which has since been changed to Marshall. Betimes the next morning we were hurrying eastward through Thoroughfare Gap of Bull Run Mountain, and late in the evening we arrived at Manassas Junction,--between Pope's army and Washington. I had read that walking was an excellent form of exercise because it brought into play every muscle of the body, and having walked nearly sixty miles in two days I was convinced that the reason assigned was valid, for the muscles of my arms and neck were almost as sore as were those of my legs. The making of long marches unexpectedly and quickly was one of the secrets of Jackson's success. It may be supposed by the uninitiated that after such fatigue the soldier is not in good condition for fighting; but the sense of weariness is lost when the excitement of battle begins.

The few Federal regiments on guard at the Junction were quickly dispersed, and trains of cars loaded with all sorts of army supplies were burned. A large building filled with commissary stores was also burned, but not before our empty haversacks had been replenished. By the light of the fires we supped plentifully on potatoes and beef and then lay down upon the ground, not to pleasant dreams, but to dreamless sleep.

On the 28th our brigade with some others went toward Centerville, in Fairfax county, and thence turning away came back into Prince William and took position on a part of the ground whereon the first battle of Manassas had been fought. Ewell's division, which had been left behind to befog Pope's mind and retard his movements, joined us and completed the defensive line of Jackson's entire corps.

The next day the Federal army began to press us vigorously, but the numerous attacks made upon us were repelled and followed by counter charges. Our Brigadier-General, Field, was wounded badly, and Company F lost some men, among whom was Lieutenant James Ball, who in the absence of Capt. William Brown was in command. By his death the control of the company was devolved upon me.

Let me here relate an incident to show that between individuals of the opposing hosts there was no animosity. During a lull in the battle I left the regiment and circumspectly proceeded forward to reconnoiter. I found in a wood a Yankee captain dangerously wounded, a fine-looking man and handsomely dressed. In reply to the question whether I could do anything for him he asked for water, and I, kneeling down, held my canteen to his lips, for which kindness he made grateful acknowledgments. "And now," said I, "there is something you can do for me: you can give me your sword, but I will not take it unless you part with it freely." He replied that I was welcome to it, for he would never need it again. After I had taken it he said: "You had better retire, because our men will soon be here again." He was thirsty, and I gave him drink; I was in danger, and he gave me friendly warning.

That sword had an unfortunate history: its beautiful scabbard, belt, and shoulder strap were ruined when my tent was burned the next winter; its hilt was shot off at Chancellorsville, and the naked blade was thrown away on that ensanguined field.

I returned to where the regiment was standing prepared to receive another attack, which, however, was not made that day. When we were ordered to fall back to our first position, I caused to be brought with us the bodies of Lieutenant Ball and his most intimate friend, Mordecai Lawson, who, like him, had been shot in the forehead. With bayonets and hands a grave was dug, in which we laid them side by side, and spreading over them a soldier's blanket, we heaped above them the turf and clods. In neither army could there have been found two braver men. Boon companions in life, in death they were not divided.

The next day, Saturday the 30th, witnessed the grand struggle that has become famous in history as the Second Battle of Manassas. After a separation of four days Longstreet's corps had come up and formed on Jackson's right, and General Pope was compelled either to retreat or fight on ground so skilfully selected by General Lee. The line of battle was nearly parallel with Bull Run, whereas in the first battle it was perpendicular to it.

There was between the two armies a bed that had been graded for a railroad, but upon which no rails have ever been laid. It was the fortune of the First Brigade to fight on Friday over a shallow cut, and on Saturday over the deepest of all. Our line being formed in an oak forest and ordered to charge, we rushed from the wood into a large field across which the cut had been dug, not knowing it was there until we came close to it. The Federal soldiers on the other side made but feeble resistance, because they had already been hotly engaged with a brigade composed of the 60th Virginia and some regiments from Louisiana. That brigade was down in the cut, having exhausted their ammunition, and it would have been captured but for our timely arrival, which filled them with rejoicing. In that charge the saber was knocked from my uplifted hand, and falling it stuck in the ground some paces behind me.

The brigade did not cross the cut, but a few of the men clambered over and I among them. There was a cannon over there which they pulled back with all the hilarity of college students, some riding astraddle the piece, cheering, and waving their caps.

We had no sooner recrossed the cut and regained our places in the line than the grand spectacle of dense columns of Pope's army coming to the assault was witnessed. In perfect array, they kept step as if on dress parade, and bore their banners proudly. I looked for a terrific shock, but before they came to close quarters with us, the Confederate artillery, massed on high ground behind us, opened upon their closed ranks, and wrought such fearful destruction as, I believe, was not dealt in any other battle of the entire war. Shells burst among them so thick and fast that in a few minutes the field was literally strewn with the killed and wounded. They halted, they turned, they fled; and Lee's whole army assuming the offensive, rushed forward and won the battle.

General Pope was going to hoist the Stars and Stripes above the capitol in Richmond, but he came no nearer to the city than Cedar Run. His men were brave, but from first to last he was mystified by Lee's superior strategy. A prisoner said to me, "If we had your Jackson, we would soon whip you." And I will express the opinion that if the Army of the Potomac had been commanded by generals who were the equals of Lee and Jackson the Southern Confederacy would have collapsed before April, 1865; and sooner still if Lee and Jackson had led the Northern armies, while the Confederates were marshaled by leaders of Pope's caliber.

CHAPTER VI

'Tis the soldiers' life
To have their balmy slumbers waked with strife.
            --SHAKESPEARE'S *Othello*.

Our next encounter with the Yankees occurred on the first day of September at a place called Ox Hill, near Chantilly on the Little River turnpike, in which they sustained a heavy loss in the death of General Philip Kearney, one of their best and bravest commanders. Inasmuch as the action took place during a thunderstorm its awful impressiveness was increased, and it was difficult to distinguish between the reverberations of the heavens and the detonations of the mimicking artillery, sometimes alternating and sometimes simultaneous.

That night, when all was still and darkness had settled upon the field where lay the victims of war, a soldier of the 40th regiment, an intrepid Irishman, George Cornwell by name, went out prowling for food and plunder, taking his musket with him. Unexpectedly meeting a Federal lieutenant and four men bearing a stretcher and searching for their wounded captain, he was asked to what regiment he belonged. With ready wit he named a New York regiment, and then learning their business and finding that they were unarmed, he leveled his musket, demanded their surrender, and brought them as prisoners within our lines. I myself did a little searching until I found a full haversack strapped to a man who would never use his teeth again. I was hungry, and chilled by the recent rain. I found in the haversack crackers and ground coffee mixed with sugar; and bringing into requisition my matches, tin cup, and canteen of water (which three things I was always careful to have about me), I soon had a pint of steaming beverage. I ate my supper, and then laid down to sleep. This was only one of many times that I slept in wet garments on the rain-soaked lap of earth without injury to my health; and the only reason I can give for the immunity is, that those were "War times."

The National army returned to Washington, and together with all the forces in and around that city was again put under the command of General McClellan.

From Chantilly we marched to the vicinity of Leesburg and went into camp near a beautiful spring, several feet deep, which was in a large square walled up with brick. The next day we came to the Potomac river, which was then about four feet deep, with its bottom covered with rounded stones of many sizes. We were not so favored as Joshua's host at the Jordan, but we just walked from shore to shore as if there were no water there. Beautiful was the scene. As I approached the river I beheld those who had crossed ascending the hill on the farther shore; in the water a double line of soldiers stretching from side to side, their guns held high above the current and gilded by the beams of the westering sun; and others behind them going down the declivity of the Virginia shore. There came unbidden to my mind some lines of one of Charles Wesley's hymns:

> One army of the living God,
> To his command we bow;
> Part of the host have crossed the flood,
> And part are crossing now.
> E'en now to their eternal home
> Some happy spirits fly;
> And we are to the margin come,
> And soon expect to die.

From Bunyan's time onward, and I know not how long before, a river has been the Christian symbol of death.

There was some expectation that when we came into Maryland many of her sons would rally to our banners, according to the prediction of a well-known song:

> "She breathes, she burns, she'll come, she'll come,
> Maryland, my Maryland;"

but the cold fact is, she did not come; and in the light of subsequent events, it is well that she did not.

From the Potomac the march was continued to the Monocacy river, near Frederick City. During our brief sojourn there we bought goods in the stores and paid for them in Confederate money, although, no doubt, the merchants would have preferred greenbacks or specie; and so far as I know nothing was taken without that remuneration.

Again Lee's army was divided, Jackson's corps being detached and sent forward for the purpose of capturing Harper's Ferry. For three days during the westward march in Maryland no rations were issued, and our only food was ears of green corn roasted or boiled without salt. These served for supper and breakfast, but we had nothing for dinner, for if when we started in the morning we put the cooked corn in the haversacks it soured under the hot rays of the sun, and time was too precious to allow a halt for cooking a fresh supply at noon.

Fording the Potomac again, we passed out of Maryland into Virginia at Williamsport and proceeded rapidly to Harper's Ferry. The Federal force occupying a very high hill which had been fortified by abattis and entrenchments, any attempt to storm it would have inflicted terrible loss upon the attacking party. With much difficulty our cannon had been placed on the Maryland Heights, on the Loudoun Heights, and on other eminences that overlooked the enemy's position; and when all was ready the order was given to the infantry to begin the assault. When we came to the foot of the little mountain occupied by the Yankees we discovered that trees had been cut so as to fall downward, and that their interlacing limbs had been trimmed and sharpened to a point. To advance upward through these innumerable spikes appeared impossible; nevertheless we began the ascent at the same time that our artillery on the mountains opened fire. The enemy, seeing our advance and being torn by plunging shots and shells from so many enfilading directions, were persuaded to surrender. As we were slowly struggling upward I looked and with a joyful feeling of relief saw the white flag flying, and a large one it was. This was on Monday, the 15th of September. So well was this affair planned by Jackson that without the loss of a man we captured 11,000 prisoners, 13,000 stand of small arms, and 73 pieces of artillery.

Having performed what was necessary to secure the fruits of this remarkable achievement, it was of the utmost importance that we should hurry away to reenforce Longstreet's corps, which was confronted by the northern army at Sharpsburg. Passing through Shepherdstown we waded the Potomac the third time. Our brigade did not reach the battle field until the evening of the 17th, when the most of the severe fighting of the day had ended. It was a drawn battle with very heavy losses on both sides. On the 18th the opposing hosts confronted each other without coming to blows. Did not McClellan blunder again? Having a much greater army, a part of which had not been engaged, ought he not to have renewed the battle in the attempt to crush the Confederates and drive them into the river? When he awoke on the 19th Lee's army was on the Virginia side.

CHAPTER VII

The midnight brought the signal-sound of strife,
The morn the marshalling in arms, the day
Battle's magnificently-stern array.
      --BYRON.

On the 20th of September McClellan sent one of his divisions over into Virginia, with the purpose, I suppose, of making a reconnoissance in force. It was attacked by the Light Division and driven back to the Maryland side of the river, not a few of the men perishing in the water. On that occasion the 47th passed within a few paces of a Yankee regiment standing in line in a field and displaying their national banner. Not a musket was fired by either party; for they, being cut off from the river, were doomed to captivity, and we were going at double quick against another force. When the engagement had ended and we were marching away, a solid shot from beyond the river ricochetted along our line and in unpleasant proximity to it. Though much of its force was spent, yet if it had struck our line it had sufficient momentum to have destroyed many lives. Here was a close call, which differed from many another in that the bounding ball was visible.

 The Maryland campaign being over, Jackson's corps retired to Bunker Hill between Winchester and Martinsburg, and there we had for more than two months an unusual season of rest and recuperation. I remember one day of special enjoyment. Obeying an order, I took a squad of men some seven or eight miles along the turnpike in the direction of Martinsburg to keep a lookout for the approach of the enemy. We halted where there was a grove on one side of the road and a dwelling-house on the other. We purchased a shoat from the matron of that domicile, who made us a stew that would have done credit to the Maypole Inn. After dinner,--the only meal worthy of that name that I had enjoyed for many months,--I took a musket, and leaving the men a short distance behind, took a stand in the middle of the road. No Yankee came in sight, but while I was there silently waiting and watching two large, beautiful wild turkeys walked with stately step across the road in easy range. Was I tempted to shoot? Yes. Did I do it? No; for I was particularly instructed that on no account must a gun be fired except on the enemy's approach. The report would have been repeated by squads in my rear, the camp would have been falsely alarmed, and I would have been justly court-martialed.

The Army of the Potomac, 100,000 strong and commanded by General Burnside, once more took up the slogan,--"On to Richmond,"--but that was more easily said than done. Before it reached the northern bank of the Rappahannock river, opposite Fredericksburg, the ever-watchful Lee, having left the valley, had occupied the heights on the other side. Jackson's corps by rapid marches arrived at Fredericksburg on the 11th of December, none too soon for the impending conflict, and took position on Longstreet's right. Nearly five miles from the town our brigade formed the extreme right of the Southern Army, which was an assignment of honor; and the 47th held the right of the brigade. The other brigades of Hill's Light Division formed on our left, Gregg's next to ours, and between the two on higher ground twenty pieces of artillery looked out across the field. Lee's army had the advantage of position, and had the rare pleasure of fighting on the defensive. It occupied the high ground that borders the river flat, and which is close to the town, but, as it continues, recedes from the river, leaving an ever widening plain. On the morning of the memorable 13th that plain resounded to the martial tread of Burnside's army.

Before the battle began General Lee, inspecting the disposition of his forces all along the line, rode up to where we stood, and dismounting from Traveller, handed the bridle-rein to an orderly. This was the first time that I saw him, and his appearance made an indelible impression upon my mind. What a noble man he was in form and face as well as in moral character! While he was examining the outlying field I had a conversation with the orderly, who spoke of the General's fondness for his horse.

Having observed that a few men of the Confederate cavalry had brought up a piece of artillery in front of our right, I obtained permission of Colonel Mayo and ran forward to join them. Two Federal batteries came forward in a gallop and in a minute's time unlimbered and began firing against Hill's division, the twenty guns of which I have spoken giving them as good as they sent and a little better. The Yankees were so hotly engaged by the firing in front of them that they paid no attention to the little cavalry gun upon the flank. The first shot did no execution, but the next struck a caisson and exploded its contents.

What more was done there I cannot say; for seeing that the Federal infantry were advancing to the charge, I hastily returned to my position in the regiment. Our men, lying in a railroad cut about two feet deep, waited until the Yankees were close upon them, and then rising up poured such volleys upon them as caused them to retire in confusion; but on our left Gregg's South Carolina brigade was broken through and he was killed. Being thereby severed from the rest of the army, we changed front and took the victorious Yankees in flank, causing them to lose their advantage and fall back to the railroad which they had crossed. Then occurred a pretty duel. The blue and the grey lines were about sixty yards apart and each was loading and firing as rapidly as possible. The Federal general and his two aides on horseback were urging their men to charge, as was evident from their gestures; but their men would not respond.

Being an officer I had no weapons but sword and pistol, but I picked up the musket of one of our men, who had loaded it but was killed before he could discharge it, and called on some of our company to shoot down the horsemen. We took deliberate aim and fired; and down went horses and riders. "Now," said I, "shoot down the colors." Four times they fell, only to be quickly raised again. I would not affirm that the little group about me shot down the horsemen and the flag, for many others were shooting at the same time; I only know that we calmly did our best in that direction. After a while the enemy turned and fled; and I was glad, for they had inflicted on the 47th a loss of fifty men in killed and wounded. However, their loss greatly exceeded ours. The next day, when a truce prevailed for burying the dead and caring for the wounded, I was informed by some of the Union soldiers that the name of that general was Jackson. He was a brave man, deserving a better fate, and he fell while nobly performing what he believed was his duty to his country.

It was the general and confident expectation that the battle would be renewed, and we were, therefore, surprised to discover on the morning of the 15th that the enemy had during the night recrossed to the northern side of the river. Their loss in the engagement was three times greater than ours. Burnside made the mistake of putting forth his greatest strength where the Confederates were strongest. If he had assailed our right as fiercely as he did our left, perhaps there might have been a different result.

In a few days after the battle I was informed by Colonel Mayo that I was "for gallant and meritorious conduct promoted to be First Lieutenant and Adjutant of the 47th regiment." I had not thought of trying to make an exhibition of unusual gallantry among so many intrepid men, but, of course, the commendation and promotion were highly gratifying.

"The love of praise, howe'er concealed by art,
Reigns more or less, and glows in ev'ry heart."

The campaign having come to an end, Lee's army went into winter quarters at camp Gregg, so named in honor of Brigadier-General Maxcy Gregg who was killed in the battle of Fredericksburg. It was near Moss Neck, the large and fertile farm of Mr. Richard Corbin. The Rappahannock river flowed between the Yankee and the Rebel armies, each picketing its own side of the stream. By common consent there was no shooting across the river, but on the other hand there was an occasional exchange of tobacco and coffee by means of little boats. We could hear them impudently singing: "O soldiers, won't you meet us." We had met them on fields of carnage, and expected to meet them again on the return of spring; but whether we should meet them "On Canaan's happy shore," or in some less pleasing locality in the eternal world, who could say?

I distinctly remember one night when my turn came to go to the river on picket duty, and the earth was covered with snow several inches deep. When my watch was off and the opportunity to sleep was afforded the question was, where to lie down. I spread on the snow some boughs that I had cut from a cedar tree and laid a gum cloth upon them. Upon this pallet I lay down and covering myself head and all with a blanket enjoyed sweet, refreshing, and healthful sleep. The next morning the blanket above my head was stiff-frozen with the moisture from my breath.

There was one man that should have been mentioned before this time,--a negro of my own age, whose name was Charles Wesley. We had grown up on the farm together, and had played, and boxed, and wrestled without respect to color. Not as a slave but as a friend he followed me to the war,--my launderer, my cook, and when I was sick, my nurse. Having orders to keep himself out of danger, he very willingly remained far in the rear when a battle was in progress, but when the firing ceased he faithfully sought me and reported for duty. While writing about Charles, I may anticipate a little and say that when we were in Pennsylvania I told him that we were on Yankee soil, and that he had the opportunity of deserting me and of remaining there as a free man. He replied that he already knew that, but that he was going to abide with me. And when I was captured at Falling Waters he had the intelligence and fidelity to ride my horse home and deliver him to my brother.

It was while we were encamped at Moss Neck that I witnessed a military execution for the offense of desertion from the 47th regiment. The criminal was on his knees, blindfolded, with his hands tied behind him to a stake. A short distance in front of him was the line of twenty men detailed to do the shooting, and commanded by an officer especially appointed. No man could tell who did the killing, for the twenty muskets were handed to them, one-half of them being loaded with blank cartridges. The rest of the regiment was drawn up, one-half on the right, and the other on the left. At the word "Fire!" the report of the guns rang out and the deserter fell forward pierced by balls. Death was instantaneous. Although the crime was mortal, the scene was painfully sad.

CHAPTER VIII

Nothing except a battle lost can be half so melancholy as a
battle won.
            --WELLINGTON.

I did not serve long as the adjutant of the 47th regiment. In March, 1863, Company I of the 40th regiment, having from one cause or another lost all its officers, unanimously desired that I should become their captain, and this desire was approved by Colonel Brockenbrough, who commanded that regiment, as well as by General Heth, who commanded the brigade. I was loath to sever connection from the regiment to which I had been attached since the beginning of the war, but I accepted the new position, because it was in the line of promotion, and the men of the company were from my native county and well known to me; moreover, I would still be in the same brigade with my old comrades of the 47th. My captain's commission was dated April 30, and was signed by James A. Seddon, Secretary of War.

When the spring had come General Joseph Hooker, the successor of unfortunate Burnside, having crossed the Rappahannock river, took up a strong position at Chancellorsville, with an army numerically twice as strong as the available Confederate forces, and declared by him to be "the finest army on the planet." At the same time a powerful detachment under General Sedgwick crossed the river below Fredericksburg and made demonstrations of attack upon the Confederate lines. Never was General Lee confronted by a more perilous situation, and never did his military genius more brilliantly appear.

In war so much depends upon the commander, that I advance the confident opinion that if the Confederates had been under the charge of Hooker and Sedgwick, and Lee and Jackson had had command of the Federal soldiers above and below Fredericksburg, the Confederate army would have been destroyed; and the Army of the Potomac would have walked straight into Richmond. That army would indeed have been "the finest on the planet," if the skill and the courage of its commander had equaled its numbers, its aggressive power, and its opulent equipment.

Hooker had a grand opportunity, but ingloriously failed to use it. He had conceived a good plan of action, and he successfully executed its initial movement; but when the decisive hour arrived his resolution failed. Instead of advancing aggressively on to Fredericksburg, as he had begun to do, he turned back and fortified his army with intrenchments. Did he mistrust himself, or his army, or both? His original scheme contemplated offensive tactics, and all its merit was sacrificed when he began to erect defensive fortifications.

Let me here briefly describe Chancellorsville and its environments as I saw them during the battle. There was no village there, but only a large brick tavern with a few outbuildings, located immediately on the north side of the road that connects Fredericksburg and Orange. In the rear it was separated from the forest by a narrow field, while in front and across the road there was a large space of open land. In the direction of Orange the road and fields declined to a wooded ravine. On the slightly elevated land in front of the tavern the Yankees had unlimbered twenty Napoleon cannon, and along the side of the ravine they had erected breastworks of logs and earth.

Late in the afternoon of Friday, May 1, our brigade had marched up from Fredericksburg and halted in striking distance of the Federal army. What could we expect but that in the morning we should be waging an assault upon its fortified position? Instead of that Jackson led us with the rest of his corps around the front of that position until we struck the road on the Orange side of Chancellorsville. We were now on Hooker's right flank, having marched quickly and silently fifteen miles over a rough and unfrequented road. The sun was sinking toward the western horizon when our lines of attack were formed on both sides of the road and at right angles to it. Immediately the onslaught began, silent, rapid, resolute, Heth's brigade being on the north or left side of the road. We had not proceeded far before we struck Howard's corps all unsuspecting and unprepared. Their fires were kindled for cooking supper, and dressed beeves were ready for distribution among the companies. They fled before us, strewing the ground with muskets, knapsacks, and other accouterments. Whoever censures them for running would probably have acted as they did, for our charge was as lightning from a cloudless sky. On the way we crossed a little farm, and as I passed the dwelling I saw several ladies who were wildly rejoicing.

When we had come within half a mile of Chancellorsville daylight had faded into night. The moon had risen, but her rays were rendered intermittent by scudding clouds. The darkness, the tangled undergrowth of the forest, and the entrenchments and artillery of the enemy combined to arrest our progress. Those cannon of which I have spoken shelled the woods in which we lay, and what a cannonade it was! The trees and bushes trembled, the air was laden with sulphurous fumes, the very earth seemed to quake under the impulse of exploding shells. There was, however, more noise than execution; only one man of my company was struck, and his broken jaw was bound up by my handkerchief.

From my position on the roadside I saw a few riderless horses running terror-stricken to the rear. These were, I believe, the animals that Jackson and his aides had ridden to the front. It is recorded that he was wounded by some soldiers of the 18th North Carolina regiment who were in the brigade of General James H. Lane. If this statement were made on less reliable authority it might be questioned; for I know that the Yankees were close to our front and that Jackson could not have ridden far beyond our line without encountering their volley. We did not hear until next morning that our peerless leader had been shot. Alas! As when Hector fell the doom of Troy was sealed, so with the death of Jackson the star of the Southern Confederacy declined.

Late in the night the firing ceased, and the Gray and the Blue lay on their arms, catching brief snatches of troubled sleep, and abiding the renewal of hostilities with the coming morning.

On the bright and pleasant Sunday that ensued no chiming bells nor melodies of sacred music were heard upon that famous field, but only the cries of antagonistic men and the horrid din of batteries and muskets. Our brigade being transferred to the right side of the road and drawn up in line of battle in the forest, it was not long before the renowned Stonewall brigade passed by us and charged upon the breastworks of the enemy. It was repulsed with heavy loss, the Yankees having preponderating advantage of position. Then Pender's intrepid brigade of North Carolinians had a similar experience. There were no braver soldiers in the army than the men composing these two defeated brigades. When, therefore, the command to charge was given to us, could we hope for a better result? As we advanced a shell struck the ground immediately before me, exploded and covered me with dirt, but providentially inflicted no wounds. Onward we rushed with the usual inspiring Rebel yell. When we came in sight of those formidable rifle pits we were delighted to find them abandoned by our foes; and when we climbed over them and entered the field just beyond them we were no less glad to discover that those batteries that had so noisily shelled us the night before had been withdrawn.

There in full view toward our left stood Chancellor's tavern, and the large field in front was literally filled with Federal soldiers in perfect array marching northward,--that is, to the rear. The retreat of Hooker's army had begun; they were not whipped but out-generaled. Passing across the road by the tavern and entering the forest behind it, they left not in sight a single blue coat, save that a battery in the tavern yard was firing upon us. Two Confederate batteries galloped up to our line, and, unlimbering, opened upon the battery in the yard at close range. There were in the Southern armies many soldiers in their teens, but here at one of the guns labored a boy who was, as I guessed from his size, not more than twelve years old. It was his part to fire the gun by pulling the lanyard, and as often as he did it he playfully rolled over backward. "Boys will be boys" even in the peril of battle. In the meantime Jeb Stuart, temporarily assigned to the command of Jackson's corps, came riding into the field, and in a spirit not unlike that of the boy was singing, "Old Joe Hooker, won't you get out the wilderness?" The Yankee battery withdrew; the battle was ended. The tavern was all ablaze, having been ignited by one of our shells,--the house that an hour before had been the headquarters of General Hooker. Our army was resting along the road in front of the burning building. As General Lee rode by, a waggish fellow of the 47th said, "General, we are too tired to cheer you this morning," and he pleasantly replied, "Well, boys, you have gotten glory enough for one day."

CHAPTER IX

He that fights and runs away
May turn and fight another day.
                              --RAY.

After the lamented death of General Jackson the divisions of the Army of Northern Virginia were organized into three corps, commanded, respectively, by Longstreet, Ewell, and A. P. Hill. General Heth was assigned to the command of the Light Division, and the senior colonel of the first brigade, John M. Brockenbrough took the command made vacant by Heth's promotion.

In forming his staff Colonel Brockenbrough selected me to be his acting assistant adjutant-general. As this new sphere of duty required that I should have a horse, and as it was useless to search for one in the neighborhood of Fredericksburg, I sought and obtained a furlough in order that I might seek one in my native county. The time was limited to five days,--not long enough, as Colonel Brockenbrough knew; but there was an understanding between us that if I overstayed the limit nothing would be said about it.

A tramp of a hundred miles was before me, but that was a matter of indifference to my buoyant body and practiced feet. It was my intention to cross the river at Tappahannock, and proceed down the Neck to my brother's home, but the southern bank was picketed by the 15th Virginia cavalry, which prohibited my passage. Walking back into the town and finding Colonel John Critcher, who was in command of the regiment, I explained my mission and requested the liberty of passing through his line. He informed me that on the other side the 8th Illinois cavalry were making a raid, and urged that I should not cross and run the risk of being captured. Telling him that I was familiar with the country and that I would avoid the enemy, I persisted in the request, being as desirous of a horse as was Richard III in his final battle. Having obtained his reluctant written permission I decided that instead of crossing at Tappahannock I would walk down as far as Owen Hill in Middlesex county and thence seek a passage over into Lancaster. A negro, whose service I secured in return for Confederate money, transported me in a canoe, and landed me at Morattico. During the passage I kept a sharp lookout up and down the wide river for Yankee gunboats, fearing that even if I should escape Scylla I might fall into Charybdis; and indeed some of the marauding bluecoats had but recently departed from the farm.

Having dined with the hospitable family, I set out for my brother's home fifteen miles away, not knowing that one part of the enemy was encamped on his farm and another part in the yard. Being informed that the hostile invaders were traversing all parts of the county in search of booty, I sought to evade them by walking not upon the familiar roads but in the woods parallel with them. When I drew near the county-seat, instead of crossing the road as prudence suggested I thought I would walk the road a short distance and then pass over, for my shoes had become uncomfortably smooth by treading on the fallen foliage of the pines. Rash procedure!

I had come into the road near what is called "the court-house mill hill," intending to go down, cross the bridge, and turn again into the woods in the rear of the village, scouting as I proceeded. When I had come nearly to the brow of the hill, I met a squadron of ascending Federal horsemen. If I had been two minutes earlier and they as much later we would have met as I was descending the hill; and then my capture would have been inevitable, because the steep banks on either side would have precluded all hope of escape. I heard the foremost riders say, "Here're the Rebels, boys; come on." I did not wait to see more than their heads and breasts as they were coming up the hill. I was in my full uniform, having a gray overcoat on my shoulder and a felt hat on my head. In the twinkling of an eye the coat was dropped, and the hat flew off as I made such a leap into the friendly forest as perhaps was never equaled by any athlete in the Olympic games. I had no time to become frightened, but I was angered by being pursued on my native soil by men who had no right to invade it. It is a wonder that they did not catch me. I heard them swearing, crying "Halt," and firing pistols. Three things favored me: the trees and undergrowth were coming into leaf, I was fleet of foot, and I took an unsuspected direction. Instead of running at right angles to the road, or obliquely backward, I ran obliquely forward, in the direction from which they had come. When I was nearly out of breath, I stopped to listen, and was glad to hear no sounds save those that were made by my thumping heart. The pursuit had ended, and I lay down to rest and to recover my wind,--not unlike the stag that had been chased by Fitz James' hounds.

In a little while rising refreshed from my rest, I went onward and crossing the mill stream higher up than I had purposed, I arrived at the residence of my cousin Robert. I had been there but a few minutes when his wife, who had glanced up the lane, cried out, "Run, run; the Yankees are coming!" At the first utterance of the word "run," I was making rapid tracks for the forest in the rear of the house; but before I reached it she called me back. Two of the Yankees had been there before, and her excited imagination had mistaken a Rebel officer for two more. It was her brother-in-law, Ned Stakes, major of the 40th Virginia. He and I then set out for a place near Wicomico church, where, as he told me, a few Confederates were in hiding. Having spent the night with them in the forest, we were in the morning informed by a faithful negro, who had been acting as commissary, that the Yankees had all gone. Although I trusted his report, it was with circumspection that I traveled homeward.

The departed Yankees had carried away teams and wagons loaded with plunder from meat-houses, barns, and cabins, and as many of the negroes as desired to take advantage of "the year of jubile?" which old Spencer said "had come." One girl, who refused to depart, was thus upbraided by her father: "You's a fool, gal, not to go where there's a plenty to eat and nothing to do." That regiment of cavalry had robbed my brother, and had treated many other peaceable citizens in the same way. Large was the booty they carried away, and long was the train of negroes, horses, and loaded wagons. It is said that "all things are lawful in war"; but this adage, like many others, sails under false colors. War is lawless, as Cicero observed: "Silent leges inter arma." There was neither constitutional nor statute law that justified the invasion of the South by armies from the North; none for the emancipation proclamation; none for the cruel and destructive deeds that were perpetrated by the Federal armies.

My furlough had run out, and my object was yet ungained. The next day I found a bay horse to my liking, five years old, large, tall, and strong, named John. The owner sold him to me for Confederate money, knowing that the sale bore close resemblance to a gift. After a night's rest I set out for the army. Riding in the wake of the retiring sons of Illinois, I recrossed the river at Bowler's, and on the second day rejoined the brigade near Fredericksburg. After having been chased by the Yankees, a feeling of safety came over me as I mingled again with my veteran companions.

That was not to be my last experience with the 8th Illinois. It was they who in less than two months afterward took me prisoner in Maryland. Some of them were riding horses that they had stolen,--no; impressed,--from my county. They showed me their repeating Spencer carbines, and asked that if I should be exchanged I would tell the 9th Virginia cavalry that they would be glad to meet them. The lapse of fifty years has made old men of them and me. I have forgiven the wrongs those brave fellows inflicted on my country, and I would be glad to meet them to talk over the stirring events of the past.

CHAPTER X

> Hand to hand, and foot to foot;
> Nothing there, save death, was mute;
> Stroke, and thrust, and flash, and cry
> For quarter, or for victory,
> Mingled with the volleying thunder.
> —BYRON.

I come now to relate my experience of the disastrous invasion of Pennsylvania.

The first week in June the commands of Longstreet and Ewell began the northward movement, but Hill's corps remained at Fredericksburg to deceive the Federal commander and watch his movements. It was not until the middle of the month that Hooker divined Lee's purpose and withdrew his army from our front, leaving us free to follow the rest of the army. Marching through Culpeper, we crossed the mountains through Chester's Gap and struck out for the ford of the Potomac at Williamsport. I had four times waded the river, but this time, being on horseback, I escaped a wetting by holding my feet high on the saddle. My spirits would not have been so light and gay, if I could have foreknown that I should not lay eyes on the river again until the war should be over. Nothing of moment occurred while we passed across Maryland into Pennsylvania.

Tuesday night, June 30, our division bivouacked near Cashtown, about eight miles northwest of Gettysburg. The next morning Colonel Brockenbrough was informed that Pettigrew's brigade was on the way to Gettysburg to obtain shoes for the men, and was ordered to follow as a support in the contingency of need, none of us knowing that the advance of Meade's army occupied a strong position between us and the town. I was riding with Colonel Brockenbrough at the head of the column when we met Pettigrew and his men returning. He informed us that the enemy was ahead and that as he had not received orders to bring on an engagement he was coming back, to report. As to the source of his information I had no doubt, for by his side was a man on horseback, bearing an umbrella, and dressed in a suit of civil clothes. After a brief consultation between the commanders of the two brigades I was ordered to ride back quickly to Heth's headquarters, report the condition of affairs, and bring back his instructions. With a brusque manner, he said, "Tell General Pettigrew not to butt too hard, or he'll butt his brains out." I translated his command into politer terms, and we started again toward Gettysburg, knowing that Heth would follow with the other four brigades of the division.

We found the enemy posted on a ridge just beyond Willoughby's Run, and deploying on both sides of the road we went into the engagement. We had the honor,--if honor it may be called,--of losing and shedding the first blood in one of the most famous battles of the world. In war things sometimes just happen: the Army of the Potomac and the Army of Northern Virginia came into collision at a place where neither commander designed a general engagement. Pender's division formed on the right of Heth's and both pressed forward in the face of volleying musketry and thundering cannon. We found out afterward that the opposing force consisted of the three divisions of the First Corps under the command of General Reynolds. Right bravely did they fight, and being driven from the ridge they formed again on Seminary Ridge, determined to hold it. As our men, on the other hand, were no less determined to take it, the contest became furious and slaughterous. Our loss was heavy, but did not equal that which we inflicted. At last they gave way, and we pursued them to the edge of the town, through the streets of which they hastened until they lodged among the rocky fastness of Cemetery Ridge. I was in all the great battles, from Seven Pines to Chancellorsville, but never had I witnessed a fight so hot and stubborn. On a field of battle the dead and mortally wounded are usually scattered promiscuously on the ground, but here I counted more than fifty fallen heroes lying in a straight line. They belonged, as well as I now remember, to the 150th Pennsylvania. When a regiment stands its ground until it suffers so great a loss, it deserves honor for its courage, for the wounded must have numbered as many as two hundred and fifty. It is a rare thing that a regiment loses so many men in one engagement.

At the same time that we were struggling with the First Corps of Meade's army the divisions of Rhodes and Early on our left were driving the Eleventh Corps before them. But of the gallant part they bore in the battle I make no mention, inasmuch as I am not writing a general history, but only jotting down the things I saw, a small part of which I was.

When the battle had ended and the brigade was standing in line close to the town, Colonel Brockenbrough and I occupied positions in rear of the line; and near us were Capt. Austin Brockenbrough and Lt. Addison Hall Crittenden. First one and then the other of these two gallant officers fell mortally wounded, although no Yankee was in sight. It was the work of sharpshooters concealed in a large wooden building on our left. I took the liberty of causing a company to fire a volley into the house and that put a stop to the murderous villainy.

It was nearly midnight when the brigade fell back a short distance to seek some rest after the severe toils of the day; but notwithstanding the lateness of the hour and our tired condition I proposed to Colonel Brockenbrough that we should look up these two men who were especially dear to us, for Austin was his cousin and Addison was mine. We knew that they had been carried on stretchers from the place where they had been wounded. Our only guides as we slowly rode along in the dark were the fires that indicated the location of the improvised hospitals of the numerous brigades. Inquiring our way, we at last came to the hospital of our brigade where Mr. Meredith, chaplain of the 47th, conducted us to our friends who were lying upon pallets of straw. They knew that their wounds were mortal, but they faced "the last enemy" with the same intrepidity they had manifested on many a sanguinary field. If I had yielded to my emotions, I would have wept over Addison even as a woman weeps. He was named for my mother's only brother; he was pure in heart; and while he was gentle and sweet in manners and disposition, he was as brave as any man who followed Lee across the Potomac.

By some critics General Lee has been censured because he did not continue the battle and attempt to capture Cemetery Ridge on the evening of the first day. I think that the criticism is unjust; for, in the first place, the attempt would have been of doubtful issue, and then if he had tried and succeeded, what advantage would have been gained? It was clearly Meade's role to act on the defensive and select the arena upon which the decisive contest must be waged. If Cemetery Ridge had been taken, instead of hurrying his other corps to that position to form a junction with the First and Eleventh, he would have retired behind Pipe Creek, or chosen some other ground as easily tenable as Cemetery Ridge. The state of things was such that Lee could not retreat without a general engagement, and he could not enter upon it except upon disadvantageous conditions. The tables were turned: as the Yankees had fought at Fredericksburg, so the Rebels had to fight in Pennsylvania.

On the second day Heth's division was not engaged, but occupied the ground near that on which it had fought the day before, close by the seminary in which General Lee had his headquarters. In the afternoon while Longstreet's corps was furiously fighting to wrest Little Round Top from the enemy, he came unattended to where I was standing. Looking down the valley of Plum Run, which separated the armies, there could be seen the flashing of the guns under the pall of smoke that covered the combatants. Now and then making a slight change of position he viewed the scene through his field-glass. His noble face was not lit up with a smile as it was when I saw it after the victory at Chancellorsville, but bore the expression of painful anxiety. Ah, if only his men could seize and hold that coveted elevation! It was the key to the situation, and victory would have been assured. But that battle was lost, although the divisions of Longstreet performed prodigies of valor. Then and there the issue was decided.

That night Heth's division moved farther to the right. Being directed by Colonel Brockenbrough to ride ahead and pick out a place for his brigade, I went forward in the darkness, ignorant of the lay of the land, until the command to halt was given to me in an undertone. I did not see the man, but was informed that I was just about to ride through the line of Confederate skirmishers, and was cautioned to ride back as quietly as I could, because the Yankee skirmishers were not far in front.

On the morning of the 3d of July, although Ewell's corps on the left had waged a bloody but unsuccessful battle, not a shot was fired by Hill's corps in the center, nor by Longstreet's on the right; but the final struggle was yet to be made. More than a hundred cannon were placed in position, along the line of which lay the eighteen thousand men, who had been selected to make the assault upon Cemetery Ridge. Before the firing began Colonel Brockenbrough told me that when the cannonading should cease we should make the charge.

About one o'clock the guns opened, and for two dreadful hours pounded the adversary's position, being answered by almost as many of his guns. There has never been such a war of artillery on the American continent. Surely this was an exhibition of the "Pride, pomp, and circumstance of glorious War." It was hoped that so terrible a bombardment would demoralize the enemy and thus prepare the way for a successful onslaught of the infantry. During its continuance we lay among the guns, and as soon as their clamor hushed sprang to our feet and began rushing toward the enemy. We had to descend the slope of Seminary Ridge, cross a valley, and ascend the steep slope of Cemetery Ridge, a distance of nearly a mile. If while we were crossing the valley the artillery behind us had been firing at the enemy over our heads, our task would have been less dangerous and more hopeful, but unwisely and unfortunately the caissons had become almost exhausted. As we were ascending the eminence, where cannon thundered in our faces and infantry four lines deep stood ready to deliver their volleys, I noticed that the line of the Confederates resembled the arc of a circle; in other words, the right and the left were more advanced than the center, and were, therefore, the first to become engaged. Brockenbrough's brigade formed the extreme left of the attacking column.

The fame of Pickett's charge on the right has resounded through the world. The Virginians on the left achieved less glory, but they did their best. We came so close to the serried ranks of the Yankees that I emptied my revolver upon them, and we were still advancing when they threw forward a column to attack our unprotected left flank. I feel no shame in recording that out of this corner the men without waiting for orders turned and fled, for the bravest soldiers cannot endure to be shot at simultaneously from the front and side. They knew that to remain, or to advance, meant wholesale death or captivity. The Yankees had a fair opportunity to kill us all, and why they did not do it I cannot tell. Our loss was less than it was in the first day's battle. As in our orderly and sullen retreat we were ascending the ridge from which we had set out, I heard the men saying mournfully, "If Old Jack had been here, it wouldn't have been like this"; and though I said nothing I entertained the same opinion.

Suppose he had been there to turn the enemy's left flank as he did at Gaines' Mill, and again at Chancellorsville!

As I look back upon that final assault at Gettysburg, it seems strange to me that General Lee should have sent eighteen thousand men to dislodge a hundred thousand from a position much stronger than that which Wellington occupied at Waterloo. Perhaps he miscalculated the effect of the cannonade; perhaps he reposed too much confidence in his soldiers. When all was over he found no fault with them, but most magnanimously took the blame of defeat upon himself and endured great mental suffering. Adverse criticism is swallowed up in sympathy for that peerless man.

It was a drawn battle. The Army of Northern Virginia had not been beaten, but it had failed in the attempt to beat the Army of the Potomac. All day long on the 4th of July it remained in view of Meade's army, but he dared not assail it.

There was nothing left but to return to Virginia. On the night of the 4th of July the army began to retreat, and on the 7th it halted near Hagerstown and offered battle, which Meade refused. It seems to me that he did not press the pursuit as closely and fiercely as he might have done; perhaps he was respecting the valor that he had lately witnessed.

CHAPTER XI

A prison is a house of care,
A place where none can thrive,
A touchstone true to try a friend,
A grave for men alive.
--Inscription on the Old Prison of Edinburg.

After falling back from Hagerstown the army took up a strong position near the Potomac, extending from Williamsport to Falling Waters. On the night of the 13th of July the retreat to Virginia began. The division of Heth and that of Pender, now commanded by Pettigrew, marched all night long in a drenching rain and over a very muddy road toward Falling Waters, where the engineers had constructed a pontoon bridge across the river. When the morning dawned we were about two miles from the river, and, so far as I know, there was no reason why we should not have kept on and followed the rest of the army over the bridge. Instead of that we halted and formed in line of battle across the road, facing northward, Heth on the right and Pettigrew on the left, well located for defense, being on rising ground and having a valley in front. It was supposed that our cavalry were between us and the enemy, (which was a false supposition,) and, contrary to well-established military rules, no skirmishers were sent to the front. The command was given to stack arms and rest, and the men exhausted by fatigue lay down on the wet ground behind the line of muskets and soon went to sleep. The guns were wet and muddy and many of them were either unloaded or unfit for action. Giving my horse to Charles to be held in the rear until called for, I too fell asleep. We were in no condition for anything except the surprise that startled us from our transitory slumbers.

We were awakened by the firing of the enemy. By the time that the muskets could be retaken from the stack, squadrons of cavalry were upon us. These were easily repulsed, not, however, until riding down in front of our line they had mortally wounded General Pettigrew at the head of his division. General Heth, riding rapidly along behind our line, was crying out, "Keep cool, men, keep cool!" But judging from the tone of his voice and his manner of riding, he seemed to me to be the only hot man on the field.

The color-bearer of the 47th exclaimed, "Come on, boys; it's nothing but cavalry," and ran forward into the valley, showing more bravery than intelligence or discipline, for infantry does not charge cavalry, and he had no right to advance without an order. The color-bearers of the other regiments of the brigades, not to be outdone, likewise advanced, and some of the bolder spirits followed their respective flags. This action was so unwise that I requested Colonel Brockenbrough to authorize me to recall these brave fellows to their original and better position; but, to my surprise, he directed me to order all the men to join their colors; and this I tried to do, but the men would not obey, saying that their muskets were unfit for action. However, I went myself, though Colonel Brockenbrough and many men of the brigade remained behind. I never saw him again.

A spirited contest ensued, which I shall dignify with the name of the battle of Falling Waters, for a real battle it was, although it is not mentioned in the histories that I have read, and the number engaged was small. On one side were portions of the four regiments of Brockenbrough's brigade, with their bullet-pierced battle flags, and on the other side were dismounted men of the 8th Illinois cavalry regiment armed with their seven-shooting carbines. There were officers present who held higher rank than mine, but, as they knew me to be of the brigade staff, they permitted me to exercise authority over the entire force. For an hour we held the Yankees in check at close quarters.

While the action was in progress I observed that one of our enemies was protected by a large tree in the field, from behind which he stepped frequently and quickly to fire upon us. As he seemed to be taking special aim at me, I requested one of our men, who had a beautiful Colt's rifle, to give me his gun, and I shot at the man the next time he emerged from behind his natural protection. He was not killed, but he darted back without shooting. I handed back the gun. Then, with my right arm around the man, I was with my left arm pointing out the enemy when he fired at us and broke the arm of my comrade that was pressed between us.

Seeing another regiment of cavalry in front, hearing their bugle sound the charge, and knowing that our ammunition was nearly exhausted, I directed all the men to retire as quickly as possible to their former position. I had not once looked back, and I supposed that the two divisions were where we had left them; but they, taking advantage of our defense, had gone across the river. All of a sudden it flashed through my mind that we could neither fight nor run. Further resistance was vain; escape, impossible. I felt angry because we had been sacrificed, and chagrined because we were about to be captured. I had known all along that I might be killed or wounded, but it had never entered my mind that I might be made a prisoner. As we were scattered upon the field and the squadrons came charging among us, a group of men gathered about me were asking, "Captain, what shall we do?" "Stand still," I replied, "and cast your muskets upon the ground." At the same time I unbuckled my useless pistol and sword and cast them from me. After we had surrendered, I regretfully record that a cavalryman discharged his pistol in our midst, but fortunately no one of us was struck. An officer, indignant at an act so cowardly and barbarous, threatened him with death if he should do the like again. That day the Yankees captured on this field and in other places about thirty-five officers and seven hundred men.

The prisoners were escorted to the rear, huddled together, and surrounded by a cordon of armed men. That night I slept with Lt. W. Peyton Moncure on the blanket of one prisoner and covered by that of the other. In the afternoon of the next day, as I was standing near the living wall that surrounded us engaged in conversation with Col. William S. Christian, of the 55th Virginia, and Capt. Lee Russell, of North Carolina, some Federal officers approached and began to talk with us. One of them was the colonel of a New York regiment, (I think it was the 122d); another was the captain of one of his companies, and another was an officer on the staff of General Meade. The Colonel invited us to take supper with him and some of his friends, and the kind and unexpected proposal was gladly accepted, for recently we had had nothing but hard-tack to satiate our hunger. At sunset he sent a guard to conduct us to his tent, which was large and comfortable. We found the table well supplied with a variety of savory eatables, and we were struck by the contrast of the tent and the table with those of the Rebels.

The Blue and the Gray gathered around that hospitable board as gleeful as boys, and as friendly as men who had been companions from childhood. The supper being ended, a polite negro who looked like an Old Virginia darky, and who acted in the two-fold capacity of cook and butler, cleared away the dishes and supplied their place with cigars and bottles of liquor of several varieties. More than once or twice the bottles passed from hand to hand, and in order to prevent drunkenness I was cautious to pour very sparingly into my tumbler. In the midst of this hilarious scene our Yankee host proposed a health to President Lincoln, which we of the Gray declined to drink; whereupon I offered to substitute a joint health to Abe Lincoln and Jeff. Davis, which they of the Blue rejected. I then proposed the toast, "The early termination of the war to the satisfaction of all concerned," and that was cordially drunk by all. It was nearly midnight when the Colonel told us that if we would promise to go back and deliver ourselves up, he would not call a guard to escort us; and we gave him our word, and bade him good night. There we were in the darkness, our limbs unfettered, our hearts longing for freedom, no Yankee eye upon us; and it is not strange that there flitted across our minds the temptation to steal away and strike out for Virginia; but though our bodies were for the moment free, our souls were bound by something stronger than manacles of steel,--our word of honor. We groped our way back, entered the circle of soldiers who were guarding our fellow-prisoners, and went to sleep on the ground, while our late entertainers reposed upon comfortable cots.

The next morning, July 16, we were hurried along by an unfeeling cavalry escort to a station near Harper's Ferry, and there put into box cars strongly guarded. On our arrival in Washington we were conducted along the streets to the Old Capitol prison. "To what vile uses" had that building come! It was superintended by a renegade Virginian, whose name I am not sorry that I have forgotten; but let me do him the justice to say that he behaved courteously and gave us a plenty to eat. The guard of the prison was the 178th New York regiment, composed of insolent Germans, some of whom could not speak the English language. I came near losing my life by the bayonet of one of them, because he could not understand a request that I made of him. The house was infested by insects whose name I will not call; but the reader will recognize their nature when I characterize them as malodorous, and blood-sucking. We could expel them from our bunks, but not from the walls and the ceiling, from the holes and the cracks of which they swarmed at night, rendering sound sleep impossible.

In a few days after having taken involuntary quarters in the Old Capitol I read with surprise and grief an article in the Baltimore *American*, headed "Meade *versus* Lee." General Lee, misinformed by somebody, had reported that there had been no battle at Falling Waters, and that none of his soldiers had been captured except those who had straggled during the night or fallen asleep in barns by the roadside. When he published that statement he knew that there had been no engagement of his ordering, but he did not know that the gallant and accomplished Pettigrew had been wounded on the field, nor that some of his men had kept the enemy in check, while others were thereby afforded the opportunity of safely crossing the river. No; the men who were captured with me were not stragglers: they were taken on the field of battle, and they were as brave and dutiful as any that ever wore the gray. Neither was General Meade's report strictly correct, but it corresponded more closely with the facts. He did not capture a brigade, as he said, but he did take the flags of Brockenbrough's brigade, and enough men of other commands to form one.

During the whole term of my imprisonment I anxiously longed to be exchanged, being willing any day to swap incarceration for the toils and dangers of active military service. In the early part of the war there were some partial exchanges, but as it was prolonged the government at Washington rejected all overtures for a cartel. Throughout the North there were raised loud and false reports that Federal soldiers in Southern prisons were being wantonly maltreated, while the National Government might have restored them to freedom and plenty by agreeing to the exchange of prisoners that was urged repeatedly by the Confederate Government. The refusal was an evidence of the straits to which the Union was pushed, and an act of injustice and cruelty to the prisoners of both sides. It was, moreover, an undesigned but exalted testimony to the valor of Southern soldiers, for it was as if Mr. Stanton, the secretary of war, had said to every man in the Federal armies: "If in the fortunes of war you should be captured, you must run the risk of death in a rebel prison. I will not give a Southern soldier for you,--you are not worth the exchange." Gen. Grant said: "Our men must suffer for the good of those who are contending with the terrible Lee;" and ignoring the claims of humanity and the usages of honorable warfare, he lowered the question to a cold commercial level when he declared that it was "cheaper to feed rebel prisoners than to fight them."

CHAPTER XII

But now we are in prison and likely long to stay,
The Yankees they are guarding us, no hope to get away;
Our rations they are scanty, 'tis cold enough to freeze,--
I wish I was in Georgia, eating goober peas.
Peas, peas, peas, peas,
Eating goober peas;
I wish I was in Georgia, eating goober peas.
      --Stanza of a Prison Song.

Only about two weeks did we abide in the Old Capitol, the officers being transported to Johnson's Island, and the privates to other prisons. Our route was by Harrisburg, and as the train was leaving the city it jumped the track, jolting horribly on the cross-ties, but inflicting no serious injury.

The Sandusky river before it passes through its narrow mouth into Lake Erie widens into a beautiful bay about four miles wide. In this bay is situated Johnson's Island, low and level, and containing three hundred acres. It is not in the middle of the bay, but is on the north side, half a mile from the main land, while on the other side it is three or more miles from the city of Sandusky across the water.

The prison walls enclosed a quadrangular space of several acres, the southern wall running along the margin of the bay and facing Sandusky. They were framed of wooden beams, on the outer side of which, three feet from the top, there was a narrow platform on which the guard kept continual watch. Thirty feet from the wall all around on the inside there was driven a row of whitewashed stobs, beyond which no prisoner was allowed to go on pain of being shot by the sentinels. At night the entire space within was illuminated by lamps and reflectors fixed against the walls.

Within the walls there were eleven large wooden buildings of uniform size, two stories high. The first four were partitioned into small rooms, and were sheathed; the remaining seven had two rooms on each floor, and they afforded no protection against the weather except the undressed clapboards that covered them. In each house the upper story was reached by an outside flight of steps. In the larger rooms some sixty or seventy men were huddled together. Around the sides bunks were framed on pieces of scantling that extended from floor to ceiling, arranged in three tiers, so that a floor space of six feet by four sufficed for six men. My cotton tick was never refilled, and after doing service for many months it became flat and hard. Our quarters and accommodations were such as the Yankees thought good enough for rebels and traitors, but in summer we were uncomfortably and unhealthily crowded, and in winter we suffered from the cold, because one stove could not warm so large and windy an apartment. Many a winter night, instead of undressing, I put an old worn overcoat over the clothes I had worn during the day.

At first I "put up" in block No. 9, afterward in No. 8, and toward the end of my imprisonment in No. 3, which was much more comfortable.

In summer, water was obtained from a shallow well, but in winter, when the bay was frozen, a few men from each mess were permitted to go out of the gate in the afternoon and dip up better water from holes cut through the ice. On these occasions a strong guard extended around the prisoners from one side of the gate to the other.

From the time of my capture until the fall of the year the rations were fairly good and sufficient, but then they were mercilessly reduced, upon the pretext of retaliation for the improper treatment of Union prisoners in the South. The bread and meat rations were diminished by a half, while coffee, sugar, candles, and other things were no longer supplied. We did our own cooking, the men of each mess taking it by turns, but the bread was baked in ovens outside and was brought in a wagon every morning. A pan of four loaves was the daily allowance for sixteen men. When I got my fourth of a loaf in the morning I usually divided it into three slices, of which one was immediately eaten and the others reserved for dinner and supper; but when the time came for the closing meal I had no bread, for hunger had previously claimed it all. But for some clothes, provisions, and money that were sent to me by kind friends residing in Kentucky and Maryland I think that I could not have lived to witness the end of the war. There was not enough nutriment in the daily ration to support vigorous health, and it was barely sufficient to sustain life. I believe that a few of the prisoners succumbed to disease and died because they had an insufficiency of nourishing food. Bones were picked from ditches, if perchance there might be upon them a morsel of meat. I was begged for bread, when I was hungry for the want of it. All the rats were eaten that could be caught in traps ingeniously contrived. When prejudice is overcome by gnawing hunger, a fat rat makes good eating, as I know from actual and enjoyable mastication.

For a time we were permitted to obtain the news of the outside world through the New York *World* and the Baltimore *Gazette*, but these were suppressed; and then we had to depend upon a little Sandusky sheet and the Baltimore *American*, which vilified the South and claimed for every battle a Union victory.

How did we while the time away? Well, we organized a minstrel band, singing clubs, and debating societies; we had occasional lectures and exchanged books in a so-called reading room; we had two rival base-ball teams, and we played the indoor games of chess, checkers, cards, and dominoes. I spent much time in reading the Bible, besides some of Scott's novels and the charming story of Picciola.

On Sunday there were Bible classes, and sometimes sermons by men who had gone from the pulpit into the army. Among them were a Methodist colonel from Missouri, a Baptist colonel from Mississippi, and a Baptist captain from Virginia. At one time evangelistic services were held in a lower room of block No. 5, and a number of converts confessed Jesus Christ as Lord and Saviour, and declared their denominational preference. Those who decided to be Baptists were permitted, under guard, to go out to the shore and were baptized in the bay by Captain Littleberry Allen, of Caroline county, Virginia; the rest could find within the walls as much water as they considered necessary for the ordinance.

Block No. 6 was set apart for a hospital, into which a prisoner might go in case of sickness. It was superintended by a Federal surgeon, but a large part of the prescribing was done by Confederate officers who had been practicing physicians. The nursing was performed by the patients' more intimate friends, who took it by turns day and night. I have a sorrowful recollection of sitting up one night to wait on Captain Scates of Westmoreland county, and to administer the medicines prescribed by the doctors. The ward was silent save for occasional groans, the lights were burning dimly, and there was no companion watching with me. About midnight the emaciated sufferer died, passing away as quietly as when one falls into healthy slumbers. I closed his eyes and remained near the body until the grateful dawn of morning. Guarded by soldiers we went to the cemetery without the walls, and committed the body to the ground, far away from his family and native land.

Nearly all the men confined on Johnson's Island were officers, of every rank from lieutenant to major-general, and numbering about twenty-six hundred. They represented all parts of the South and nearly every occupation, whether manual or professional. They were men of refinement,--ingenious, daring; and they were enclosed in this prison because it was secured no less by an armed guard than by the surrounding water.

Every man was trying to devise some method of escape, but only a few succeeded, not only because the difficulty was great, but also because there were spies among us. Three men tunneled out from Block No. 1, only to find themselves surrounded by Yankee soldiers. Captain Cole, a portly man, became jammed in the passage, and was somewhat like Abe Lincoln's ox that was caught and held on a fence, unable to kick one way or gore the other. The incident furnished the theme of another minstrel song, with the chorus, "If you belong to Gideon's band."

I had a secret agreement with Captain John Stakes, of the 40th Virginia, that if either saw a way of escape he would let the other know. Many a time with longing eyes we looked upon a sloop that used to tie up for the night at a wharf near the island. If we only could get to it! And so we began a tunnel under block No. 9, but finding that our labors were discovered by a spy, we were constrained to desist.

Two men filed saw teeth on the backs of case knives, and on a rainy, dark, and windy night they crawled down a ditch to the wall on the bay shore, and cut their way out; but they were captured and brought back.

There were a few successful escapes. One man, smarter than the rest of us, when we went to a vessel to fill our ticks with straw concealed himself under what remained in the hold and was carried back to Sandusky, whence he wended his stealthy flight. Colonel B. L. Farinholt, of Virginia, got away in a very artful manner, an account of which has been published. In January, 1865, when the thermometer registered 15 deg. below zero and an arctic northwest wind was blowing furiously Captain Stakes took me aside and told me in whispers that he and five others were going out that night, and that they had agreed that I might go with them. I answered that if the Yankees were to throw open all the gates and grant permission, I would not in my feeble health and with clothes so insufficient, depart in such bitter weather. When the hour came those six men rushed to the wall, and setting up against it a bench, on which rungs had been nailed, climbed over. They were not shot at, perhaps because the sentries, not expecting such an attempt, had taken refuge from the cold in their boxes. On the thick ice that begirt the island they crossed over on the north side and gained the mainland. Captain Robinson, of Westmoreland, and three others with him, hiding in the daytime and traveling at night, after enduring many hardships arrived in Canada, where they were clothed and fed and supplied with money. Taking shipping at Halifax, they ran the blockade and landed in Wilmington, North Carolina. One of the six men was recaptured by a detective on a train in New York. My friend Stakes was overtaken the next morning and brought back so badly frostbitten that it became necessary to amputate parts of some of his fingers.

By some means, I know not how, information was received in the prison that certain agents of the Confederate government in Canada would come to the island in steamboats captured on Lake Erie to release the prisoners. It was agreed that when they approached and blew a horn the prisoners would storm the walls and overpower the guards. We, therefore, organized ourselves into companies and regiments and waited anxiously for the sight of the boats and the sound of the horn. Though we had no arms, except such as the rage of the moment might supply, and did not doubt that some of us would be killed, we were ready to fulfil our part of the desperate contract; and we felt no doubt of success, for the Hoffman Battalion that composed our guard had never been in battle nor heard the rebel yell. The expected rescuers never came. There must have been some real foundation for the proposed movement, for very soon the guard was reinforced by a veteran brigade, and the gunboat *Michigan* came and anchored near the island and showed her threatening portholes.

CHAPTER XIII

> 'Mid pleasures and palaces though we may roam,
> Be it ever so humble, there's no place like home;
> A charm from the skies seems to hallow us there,
> Which seek through the world, is ne'er met with elsewhere.
> --PAYNE.

If one longs for home while roaming amidst pleasures and palaces, how much more intense, suppose you, must be the nostalgia of the soldier confined in a far distant prison?

March 14, 1865, was one of the happiest days of my life. After a captivity of twenty months, I was led out of the prison with the three hundred others, conducted to a steamboat, and homeward bound transported to Sandusky. The thick ice that for three months had covered the bay was floating in broken pieces on the surface, through which the boat struggled with so much difficulty that I feared it would be necessary to put back to the island; but the trip was made at the expense of some broken paddles. Why we were selected rather than our less fortunate compatriots I cannot guess, unless it was to save the annoyance and the expense of burial, for some of our party had been wounded, others as well as myself, had recently recovered from serious sickness, and all were adjudged to be unfit for military service; or perhaps there was the same number in Southern prisons that for special reasons the Federal War Office desired to have exchanged.

The train that was to convey us southward was made up of box-cars, upon the floors of which there was a thin covering of straw. We were so crowded that we all could not lie down at the same time. The sleepers lay with their heads at the sides of the cars, while their legs interlaced in the middle. We took the situation in good humor, and slept by turns, those who could not find room standing amidst entangled legs and feet. Thus we traveled several days and nights, our train being frequently switched for the passage of regular trains. Our route was by Bellaire to Baltimore, or rather to Locust Point, where we took passage on a steamboat for James river. Having landed the next day, we walked across a neck of land formed by a bend of the river to the wharf where a boat from Richmond was expected to meet us. A company of negroes made a show of conducting us across the neck, though a company of children armed with cornstalks would have been equally efficient.

We had not long to wait until the smokestack of the Confederate steamboat could be seen winding along as she tracked the serpentine course of the river. As she neared the wharf the band on board struck up that sweetest of tunes,--"Home, Sweet Home." Some of my companions laughed, some threw their caps into the air, others hurrahed, while my own emotions were expressed only by tears of joy that coursed down my cheeks. When, however, the music glided into the exhilarating notes of "Dixie" I joined in the cheering that mingled with the strain.

We arrived in Richmond on the 22d of March, the eighth day after we had started. I was pained to notice in the city so many signs of delapidation and poverty, and to learn that Confederate money had depreciated to the point of sixty for one. The captain's salary that the government owed me for two years was worth only about fifty dollars in specie, which a friend in the treasury department advised me to collect at once, inasmuch as he thought that the capital would be soon evacuated. I took him for a timorous prophet, and told him I would wait until I rejoined the army, when I should need it. I did not know, as he did, the impoverished and critical condition of the Confederacy.

I was not exchanged, but "paroled for thirty days unless sooner exchanged." I set out for the Northern Neck in company with Lieutenant Purcell, of Richmond county, and Captain Stakes, of Northumberland. We rode on a train as far as Hanover and then struck out afoot across the country. Notwithstanding the fact that one of my companions limped on a leg that had been wounded at Gettysburg and the other was a little lame from frosted toes, it taxed all my powers to keep up with them. If I had rejoiced to see the James, I was happier still to set foot once more upon the bank of the Rappahannock. When we had crossed over we went to the home of Lieutenant Purcell, where we spent the night, and the next day, Monday, March 27, I arrived at home. I supposed that I should take them by surprise, but somehow they had received intelligence of my coming; and as I approached the house I found them all lined up in the yard, white and black. "And they began to be merry."

I found John in the stable, having been ridden home by my faithful man, Charles Wesley, who supposed that he had left me dead at Falling Waters.

On the 14th of April, Good Friday, when I was thinking of returning to Richmond to inquire whether I had been exchanged and was still hoping for the independence of the Southern Confederacy, I attended religious services at a church in the neighborhood. When these had been concluded and the congregation were talking as usual in the yard a messenger arrived with a newspaper, which the Yankees had sent ashore from one of their gunboats, and which contained the details of General Lee's surrender of his army five days previously at Appomattox. My heart sank within me. My fondest hopes were crushed. The cause for which I had so often exposed my life, and for which so many of my friends had died, had sunk into the gloomy night of defeat.

I was thankful that out of the horrid conflict I had escaped with my life, a gray coat, and a silver quarter of a dollar. Although I had participated in all the battles that were fought by the Army of Northern Virginia, I was never seriously hurt. At Manassas one bullet struck my leg, and another forcibly wrenched my sword from my hand. At Chancellorsville a bomb exploded just in front of me, making a hole in the ground and covering me with dirt, the pieces flying away with discordant noises. Countless balls whizzed by my ears, and men fell all around me, some of them while touching my side. Am I not justified in appropriating the words of David addressed to Jehovah, "Thou hast covered my head in the day of battle?"

Withdrawal from the Union was the right of the Southern States, as appears from the history of the making and adoption of the federal constitution; and great was the provocation to use it. It is not, however, always wise,--either for persons or communities,--to exercise their rights. Secession in the year 1860 was a hot headed and stupendous political blunder,--a blunder recognized by the majority of the people of Virginia, who refused to follow the example of her southern sisters until there was forced upon her the cruel alternative of waging war either against them or against the States of the North.

Though secession was a grievous error, nevertheless the war that was waged by the Federal Government was a crime against the constitution, humanity, and God. But now, as we view the present and retrospect the past, who may say that all has not turned out for the best? We find consolation in the belief that the Lord's hand has shaped our destiny, and we meekly submit to his overruling providence.

"If it were done, when 'tis done, then 'twere well   It were done quickly."

But the war, like Duncan's murder, was not done after it was done. There supervened the unnecessary, vindictive, and malignant reconstruction acts of the Federal Congress.

On the 14th of April, only nine days after Lee had surrendered, a great calamity befell the South in the foolish and infamous assassination of President Lincoln, who was the only man who could have restrained the rage of such men as Sumner in the Senate and Stephens in the House of Representatives. The hatred of the Northern politicians was intensified by the supposition that his death was instigated by Southern men, and it did not abate even after they were convinced that the supposition was unfounded.

It is a singular fact that while the war was in progress the acts of secession were considered null and void, and the Southern States were declared to be parts of an indissoluble union, but when the war had ended they were dealt with as alien commonwealths and conquered territories. For four years Virginia was not a co-equal State in the Union but "Military District No. 1," governed by a Federal general, who appointed the local officers in the several counties. The affairs of the State were managed by carpetbaggers in close agreement with despicable scalawags and ignorant negroes. The elective franchise was granted to the emancipated slaves regardless of character or intelligence, while it was denied to many white men. In Lancaster county the negroes had a registered majority of a hundred voters; it was represented in a constitutional convention by a carpetbagger, and after the adoption of the constitution it was represented in the Legislature by a negro. To injury were added hatred and insult. It was not enough that the South was conquered, it must be humiliated by African domination!

The Southern people did not go to war--war came to them. Not to gain military glory did they fight, although this meed must be awarded to them. Nor was the perpetuation of African slavery the object for which they took up arms, for in Virginia nineteen-twentieths of the citizens owned no slaves, and there was perhaps the same proportion in the other States of the Confederacy. Neither was it for conquest that they so long waged the unequal contest; for though they twice crossed the Potomac it was not to gain an acre of territory, but only to relieve their own beleaguered capital. From first to last it was a purely defensive struggle to maintain for themselves the freedom they cheerfully accorded to other communities, and to make good the inherited belief that "all just government derives its power from the consent of the governed." They simply resisted subjugation by a hostile government whose right to rule them they denied.

As we review the history of that gigantic struggle we are not surprised that the South was subdued, the only wonder being that it was not sooner done. It required two and a quarter millions of soldiers four years to overcome one-third of that number. The South had no navy to open her ports, no commerce for her products, no foundries for the manufacture of arms. During the first year there were not muskets enough to supply her volunteers, though later on sufficient numbers were taken on the fields of battles, fifty-two cannon and thirty thousand small arms being captured in the battles around Richmond, besides the many thousands that were taken in subsequent engagements.

That the South for so long a time resisted the attempts of her powerful enemy, and during that period gained so many remarkable victories, is attributable to the skill of her generals and the valor of her soldiers. In these respects only was the advantage on her side.

The fame of her generals has spread throughout the world, and their campaigns enrich the text-books of the military students of Europe and Asia. They rank with the most famous commanders that ever led armies to victory. Their names are immortal, and their memory is enshrined not only in poetry and history, in marble and bronze, but also in the admiration of mankind and in the affections of the Southern people.

But what could strategy have achieved unless there had been soldiers to make it effective? The men had confidence in their commanders and were responsive to their genius. In attack they exhibited impulsive courage, and in defense possessed unyielding firmness. They made days and places forever historic, when their pay was money in little more than name, their garments torn, their rations coarse and scant. Footsore they charged against the dense Blue lines, or made those rapid marches that bewildered opposing forces.

When the end had come both officers and men surrendered as they had fought,--without mental reservation. Sadly they furled and yielded up the bullet-riddled battleflags they had carried so proudly. Now while they manfully accept the hard arbitrament of war, and yield unaffected loyalty to the United States, they make no confession of criminality. While the war continued they were asserting what they believed was a God-given right, and now they recall with pride the valor and victories of the Southern armies.

Those armies are rapidly disappearing from the land they loved so well. Many of the men fell in battle, and many died in prisons and hospitals, and since the close of the war more of them have fallen asleep in peaceful homes. Those who have departed and those who survive will not want a eulogist while one remains; and when the last of the men who wore the gray shall have joined his comrades beyond the river of death, coming generations will celebrate their heroism and scatter flowers upon the mounds that mark the places where their ashes repose.

www.bookjungle.com *email: sales@bookjungle.com fax: 630-214-0564 mail: Book Jungle PO Box 2226 Champaign, IL 61825*

The Codes Of Hammurabi And Moses
W. W. Davies

QTY

The discovery of the Hammurabi Code is one of the greatest achievements of archaeology, and is of paramount interest, not only to the student of the Bible, but also to all those interested in ancient history...

Religion   **ISBN:** *1-59462-338-4*   **Pages:**132
MSRP $12.95

The Theory of Moral Sentiments
Adam Smith

QTY

This work from 1749. contains original theories of conscience amd moral judgment and it is the foundation for systemof morals.

Philosophy   **ISBN:** *1-59462-777-0*   **Pages:**536
MSRP $19.95

Jessica's First Prayer
Hesba Stretton

QTY

In a screened and secluded corner of one of the many railway-bridges which span the streets of London there could be seen a few years ago, from five o'clock every morning until half past eight, a tidily set-out coffee-stall, consisting of a trestle and board, upon which stood two large tin cans, with a small fire of charcoal burning under each so as to keep the coffee boiling during the early hours of the morning when the work-people were thronging into the city on their way to their daily toil...

Childrens   **ISBN:** *1-59462-373-2*   **Pages:**84
MSRP $9.95

My Life and Work
Henry Ford

QTY

Henry Ford revolutionized the world with his implementation of mass production for the Model T automobile. Gain valuable business insight into his life and work with his own auto-biography... "We have only started on our development of our country we have not as yet, with all our talk of wonderful progress, done more than scratch the surface. The progress has been wonderful enough but..."

Biographies/   **ISBN:** *1-59462-198-5*   **Pages:**300
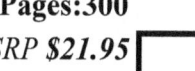
MSRP $21.95

www.bookjungle.com *email: sales@bookjungle.com fax: 630-214-0564 mail: Book Jungle PO Box 2226 Champaign, IL 61825*

The Art of Cross-Examination
Francis Wellman

QTY

I presume it is the experience of every author, after his first book is published upon an important subject, to be almost overwhelmed with a wealth of ideas and illustrations which could readily have been included in his book, and which to his own mind, at least, seem to make a second edition inevitable. Such certainly was the case with me; and when the first edition had reached its sixth impression in five months, I rejoiced to learn that it seemed to my publishers that the book had met with a sufficiently favorable reception to justify a second and considerably enlarged edition. ..

Reference   **ISBN:** *1-59462-647-2*   **Pages:412** **MSRP $19.95**

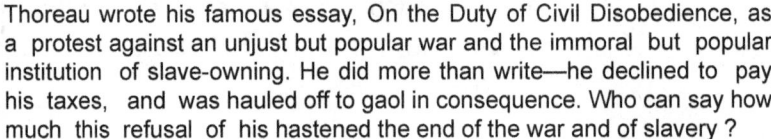

On the Duty of Civil Disobedience
Henry David Thoreau

QTY

Thoreau wrote his famous essay, On the Duty of Civil Disobedience, as a protest against an unjust but popular war and the immoral but popular institution of slave-owning. He did more than write—he declined to pay his taxes, and was hauled off to gaol in consequence. Who can say how much this refusal of his hastened the end of the war and of slavery ?

Law   **ISBN:** *1-59462-747-9*   **Pages:48** **MSRP $7.45**

Dream Psychology Psychoanalysis for Beginners
Sigmund Freud

QTY

Sigmund Freud, born Sigismund Schlomo Freud (May 6, 1856 - September 23, 1939), was a Jewish-Austrian neurologist and psychiatrist who co-founded the psychoanalytic school of psychology. Freud is best known for his theories of the unconscious mind, especially involving the mechanism of repression; his redefinition of sexual desire as mobile and directed towards a wide variety of objects; and his therapeutic techniques, especially his understanding of transference in the therapeutic relationship and the presumed value of dreams as sources of insight into unconscious desires.

Psychology   **ISBN:** *1-59462-905-6*   **Pages:196** **MSRP $15.45**

The Miracle of Right Thought
Orison Swett Marden

QTY

Believe with all of your heart that you will do what you were made to do. When the mind has once formed the habit of holding cheerful, happy, prosperous pictures, it will not be easy to form the opposite habit. It does not matter how improbable or how far away this realization may see, or how dark the prospects may be, if we visualize them as best we can, as vividly as possible, hold tenaciously to them and vigorously struggle to attain them, they will gradually become actualized, realized in the life. But a desire, a longing without endeavor, a yearning abandoned or held indifferently will vanish without realization.

Self Help   **ISBN:** *1-59462-644-8*   **Pages:360** **MSRP $25.45**

www.bookjungle.com *email: sales@bookjungle.com fax: 630-214-0564 mail: Book Jungle PO Box 2226 Champaign, IL 61825*

QTY

- **The Rosicrucian Cosmo-Conception Mystic Christianity** *by Max Heindel*   ISBN: *1-59462-188-8*   **$38.95**
  The Rosicrucian Cosmo-conception is not dogmatic, neither does it appeal to any other authority than the reason of the student. It is; not controversial, but is: sent forth in the, hope that it may help to clear...   New Age/Religion Pages 646

- **Abandonment To Divine Providence** *by Jean-Pierre de Caussade*   ISBN: *1-59462-228-0*   **$25.95**
  "The Rev. Jean Pierre de Caussade was one of the most remarkable spiritual writers of the Society of Jesus in France in the 18th Century. His death took place at Toulouse in 1751. His works have gone through many editions and have been republished...   Inspirational/Religion Pages 400

- **Mental Chemistry** *by Charles Haanel*   ISBN: *1-59462-192-6*   **$23.95**
  Mental Chemistry allows the change of material conditions by combining and appropriately utilizing the power of the mind. Much like applied chemistry creates something new and unique out of careful combinations of chemicals the mastery of mental chemistry...   New Age Pages 354

- **The Letters of Robert Browning and Elizabeth Barret Barrett 1845-1846 vol II**   ISBN: *1-59462-193-4*   **$35.95**
  by Robert Browning and Elizabeth Barrett   Biographies Pages 596

- **Gleanings In Genesis (volume I)** *by Arthur W. Pink*   ISBN: *1-59462-130-6*   **$27.45**
  Appropriately has Genesis been termed "the seed plot of the Bible" for in it we have, in germ form, almost all of the great doctrines which are afterwards fully developed in the books of Scripture which follow...   Religion/Inspirational Pages 420

- **The Master Key** *by L. W. de Laurence*   ISBN: *1-59462-001-6*   **$30.95**
  In no branch of human knowledge has there been a more lively increase of the spirit of research during the past few years than in the study of Psychology, Concentration and Mental Discipline. The requests for authentic lessons in Thought Control, Mental Discipline and...   New Age/Business Pages 422

- **The Lesser Key Of Solomon Goetia** *by L. W. de Laurence*   ISBN: *1-59462-092-X*   **$9.95**
  This translation of the first book of the "Lernegton" which is now for the first time made accessible to students of Talismanic Magic was done, after careful collation and edition, from numerous Ancient Manuscripts in Hebrew, Latin, and French...   New Age/Occult Pages 92

- **Rubaiyat Of Omar Khayyam** *by Edward Fitzgerald*   ISBN: *1-59462-332-5*   **$13.95**
  Edward Fitzgerald, whom the world has already learned, in spite of his own efforts to remain within the shadow of anonymity, to look upon as one of the rarest poets of the century, was born at Bredfield, in Suffolk, on the 31st of March, 1809. He was the third son of John Purcell...   Music Pages 172

- **Ancient Law** *by Henry Maine*   ISBN: *1-59462-128-4*   **$29.95**
  The chief object of the following pages is to indicate some of the earliest ideas of mankind, as they are reflected in Ancient Law, and to point out the relation of those ideas to modern thought.   Religion/History Pages 452

- **Far-Away Stories** *by William J. Locke*   ISBN: *1-59462-129-2*   **$19.45**
  "Good wine needs no bush, but a collection of mixed vintages does. And this book is just such a collection. Some of the stories I do not want to remain buried for ever in the museum files of dead magazine-numbers an author's not unpardonable vanity..."   Fiction Pages 272

- **Life of David Crockett** *by David Crockett*   ISBN: *1-59462-250-7*   **$27.45**
  "Colonel David Crockett was one of the most remarkable men of the times in which he lived. Born in humble life, but gifted with a strong will, an indomitable courage, and unremitting perseverance...   Biographies/New Age Pages 424

- **Lip-Reading** *by Edward Nitchie*   ISBN: *1-59462-206-X*   **$25.95**
  Edward B. Nitchie, founder of the New York School for the Hard of Hearing, now the Nitchie School of Lip-Reading, Inc, wrote "LIP-READING Principles and Practice". The development and perfecting of this meritorious work on lip-reading was an undertaking...   How-to Pages 400

- **A Handbook of Suggestive Therapeutics, Applied Hypnotism, Psychic Science**   ISBN: *1-59462-214-0*   **$24.95**
  by Henry Munro   Health/New Age/Health/Self-help Pages 376

- **A Doll's House: and Two Other Plays** *by Henrik Ibsen*   ISBN: *1-59462-112-8*   **$19.95**
  Henrik Ibsen created this classic when in revolutionary 1848 Rome. Introducing some striking concepts in playwriting for the realist genre, this play has been studied the world over.   Fiction/Classics/Plays 308

- **The Light of Asia** *by sir Edwin Arnold*   ISBN: *1-59462-204-3*   **$13.95**
  In this poetic masterpiece, Edwin Arnold describes the life and teachings of Buddha. The man who was to become known as Buddha to the world was born as Prince Gautama of India but he rejected the worldly riches and abandoned the reigns of power when...   Religion/History/Biographies Pages 170

- **The Complete Works of Guy de Maupassant** *by Guy de Maupassant*   ISBN: *1-59462-157-8*   **$16.95**
  "For days and days, nights and nights, I had dreamed of that first kiss which was to consecrate our engagement, and I knew not on what spot I should put my lips..."   Fiction/Classics Pages 240

- **The Art of Cross-Examination** *by Francis L. Wellman*   ISBN: *1-59462-309-0*   **$26.95**
  Written by a renowned trial lawyer, Wellman imparts his experience and uses case studies to explain how to use psychology to extract desired information through questioning.   How-to/Science/Reference Pages 408

- **Answered or Unanswered?** *by Louisa Vaughan*   ISBN: *1-59462-248-5*   **$10.95**
  Miracles of Faith in China   Religion Pages 112

- **The Edinburgh Lectures on Mental Science (1909)** *by Thomas*   ISBN: *1-59462-008-3*   **$11.95**
  This book contains the substance of a course of lectures recently given by the writer in the Queen Street Hall, Edinburgh. Its purpose is to indicate the Natural Principles governing the relation between Mental Action and Material Conditions...   New Age/Psychology Pages 148

- **Ayesha** *by H. Rider Haggard*   ISBN: *1-59462-301-5*   **$24.95**
  Verily and indeed it is the unexpected that happens! Probably if there was one person upon the earth from whom the Editor of this, and of a certain previous history, did not expect to hear again...   Classics Pages 380

- **Ayala's Angel** *by Anthony Trollope*   ISBN: *1-59462-352-X*   **$29.95**
  The two girls were both pretty, but Lucy who was twenty-one who supposed to be simple and comparatively unattractive, whereas Ayala was credited, as her Bombwhat romantic name might show, with poetic charm and a taste for romance. Ayala when her father died was nineteen...   Fiction Pages 484

- **The American Commonwealth** *by James Bryce*   ISBN: *1-59462-286-8*   **$34.95**
  An interpretation of American democratic political theory. It examines political mechanics and society from the perspective of Scotsman James Bryce   Politics Pages 572

- **Stories of the Pilgrims** *by Margaret P. Pumphrey*   ISBN: *1-59462-116-0*   **$17.95**
  This book explores pilgrims religious oppression in England as well as their escape to Holland and eventual crossing to America on the Mayflower, and their early days in New England...   History Pages 268

www.bookjungle.com email: sales@bookjungle.com fax: 630-214-0564 mail: Book Jungle PO Box 2226 Champaign, IL 61825

Title	ISBN	Price	QTY
The Fasting Cure *by Sinclair Upton* — In the Cosmopolitan Magazine for May, 1910, and in the Contemporary Review (London) for April, 1910, I published an article dealing with my experiences in fasting. I have written a great many magazine articles, but never one which attracted so much attention... *New Age/Self Help/Health Pages 164*	*1-59462-222-1*	$13.95	
Hebrew Astrology *by Sepharial* — In these days of advanced thinking it is a matter of common observation that we have left many of the old landmarks behind and that we are now pressing forward to greater heights and to a wider horizon than that which represented the mind-content of our progenitors... *Astrology Pages 144*	*1-59462-308-2*	$13.45	
Thought Vibration or The Law of Attraction in the Thought World *by William Walker Atkinson* — *Psychology/Religion Pages 144*	*1-59462-127-6*	$12.95	
Optimism *by Helen Keller* — Helen Keller was blind, deaf, and mute since 19 months old, yet famously learned how to overcome these handicaps, communicate with the world, and spread her lectures promoting optimism. An inspiring read for everyone... *Biographies/Inspirational Pages 84*	*1-59462-108-X*	$15.95	
Sara Crewe *by Frances Burnett* — In the first place, Miss Minchin lived in London. Her home was a large, dull, tall one, in a large, dull square, where all the houses were alike, and all the sparrows were alike, and where all the door-knockers made the same heavy sound... *Childrens/Classic Pages 88*	*1-59462-360-0*	$9.45	
The Autobiography of Benjamin Franklin *by Benjamin Franklin* — The Autobiography of Benjamin Franklin has probably been more extensively read than any other American historical work, and no other book of its kind has had such ups and downs of fortune. Franklin lived for many years in England, where he was agent... *Biographies/History Pages 332*	*1-59462-135-7*	$24.95	

Name	
Email	
Telephone	
Address	
City, State ZIP	

☐ Credit Card   ☐ Check / Money Order

Credit Card Number	
Expiration Date	
Signature	

Please Mail to: Book Jungle
PO Box 2226
Champaign, IL 61825
or Fax to: 630-214-0564

ORDERING INFORMATION

web: *www.bookjungle.com*
email: *sales@bookjungle.com*
fax: *630-214-0564*
mail: *Book Jungle PO Box 2226 Champaign, IL 61825*
or PayPal *to sales@bookjungle.com*

Please contact us for bulk discounts

DIRECT-ORDER TERMS

20% Discount if You Order Two or More Books
Free Domestic Shipping!
Accepted: Master Card, Visa, Discover, American Express

www.ingramcontent.com/pod-product-compliance
Lightning Source LLC
Chambersburg PA
CBHW081328040426
42453CB00013B/2332